MODERN NOVELISTS

General Editor: Norman Page

MODERN NOVELISTS

Published titles

ALBERT CAMUS   Philip Thody
FYODOR DOSTOEVSKY   Peter Conradi
WILLIAM FAULKNER   David Dowling
GUSTAVE FLAUBERT   David Roe
E. M. FORSTER   Norman Page
WILLIAM GOLDING   James Gindin
GRAHAM GREENE   Neil McEwan
CHRISTOPHER ISHERWOOD   Stephen Wade
HENRY JAMES   Alan Bellringer
JAMES JOYCE   Richard Brown
D. H. LAWRENCE   G. M. Hyde
DORIS LESSING   Ruth Whittaker
MALCOLM LOWRY   Tony Bareham
GEORGE ORWELL   Valerie Meyers
ANTHONY POWELL   Neil McEwan
MARCEL PROUST   Philip Thody
BARBARA PYM   Michael Cotsell
SIX WOMEN NOVELISTS   Merryn Williams
MURIEL SPARK   Norman Page
JOHN UPDIKE   Judie Newman
EVELYN WAUGH   Jacqueline McDonnell
H. G. WELLS   Michael Draper
VIRGINIA WOOLF   Edward Bishop

Forthcoming titles

MARGARET ATWOOD   Coral Ann Howells
SAUL BELLOW   Peter Hyland
IVY COMPTON-BURNETT   Janet Godden
JOSEPH CONRAD   Owen Knowles
GEORGE ELIOT   Alan Bellringer
F. SCOTT FITZGERALD   John Whitley
JOHN FOWLES   James Acheson
ERNEST HEMINGWAY   Peter Messent
NORMAN MAILER   Michael Glenday
THOMAS MANN   Martin Travers
V. S. NAIPAUL   Bruce King
PAUL SCOTT   G. K. Das
PATRICK WHITE   Mark Williams

MODERN NOVELISTS
JAMES JOYCE

Richard Brown

St. Martin's Press   New York

All rights reserved. For information, write:
Scholarly and Reference Division,
St. Martin's Press, Inc., 175 Fifth Avenue,
New York, N.Y. 10010

First published in the United States of America in 1992

Printed in Hong Kong

ISBN 0–312–06887–5

Library of Congress Cataloging-in-Publication Data
Brown, Richard, 1954–
    James Joyce / Richard Brown.
        p.   cm.—(Modern novelists)
    Includes bibliographical references and index.
    ISBN 0–312–06887–5
    1. James Joyce, 1882–1941—Criticism and interpretation.
    I. Title.   II. Series.
PR6019.097526344   1992
823'.912—dc20   91–27199
                                                          CIP

For William, Charlotte and Arthur

Contents

List of Tables

Acknowledgements

For permission to quote from the works of James Joyce I am indebted to the Society of Authors on behalf of the James Joyce Estate. I am also grateful to the School of English at the University of Leeds for the term of study leave during which this book was completed.

I would by no means proceed without offering my thanks to my editorial colleagues and contributors to the *James Joyce Broadsheet* who have helped in many ways, and to my colleagues and students at the University of Leeds whose alert curiosities have helped to direct my sense of what one should and should not want to know about Joyce. To members of the James Joyce Research Group at Leeds and to others, particularly to those (Alistair Stead, Pieter Bekker and Bryan Cheyette) who agreed to read drafts of chapters, grateful thanks are due. Needless to say the inadequacies of what follows are all my own. I thank the students who participated in the Nighttown Theatre project *Ce Bordel* which forced me to discipline my attention to the 'Circe' episode of *Ulysses* in new ways. I am indebted to the editors of a number of collections of essays where some threads of the argument may have appeared in earlier versions. My thanks, as ever, also go to Jane who is an actuality to set against my own 'possibility theory'.

List of Abbreviations

Below is a list of Joyce's works in standard editions with their usual abbreviations. Page numbers used in the text are references to these editions. Where necessary in *Ulysses* episode and line numbers as well as page references are given. For the benefit of readers unfamiliar with the book I have also on occasion used numbers of episodes in brackets. For *Finnegans Wake* page and line numbers are used throughout.

D	*Dubliners*, ed. Robert Scholes (London: Cape, 1969).
E	*Exiles* (London: Cape, 1952).
FW	*Finnegans Wake* (London: Faber, 1939).
GJ	*Giacomo Joyce*, ed. Richard Ellmann (London: Faber, 1968).
JJA	*The James Joyce Archive*, ed. Michael Groden *et al.* (New York: Garland, 1978).
LI	*The Letters of James Joyce*, vol. I, ed. Stuart Gilbert (London: Faber, 1957).
LII/III	*The Letters of James Joyce*, vols II and III, ed. Richard Ellmann (London: Faber, 1966).
P	*A Portrait of the Artist as a Young Man*, ed. Chester Anderson (London: Cape, 1968).
SH	*Stephen Hero*, ed. Theodore Spencer (London: Cape, 1956).
SL	*Selected Letters of James Joyce*, cd. Richard Ellmann (London: Faber, 1975).
U	*Ulysses* (London: Penguin, 1986).

General Editor's Preface

The death of the novel has often been announced, and part of the secret of its obstinate vitality must be its capacity for growth, adaptation, self-renewal and self-transformation: like some vigorous organism in a speeded-up Darwinian ecosystem, it adapts itself quickly to a changing world. War and revolution, economic crisis and social change, radically new ideologies such as Marxism and Freudianism, have made this century unprecedented in human history in the speed and extent of change, but the novel has shown an extraordinary capacity to find new forms and techniques and to accommodate new ideas and conceptions of human nature and human experience, and even to take up new positions on the nature of fiction itself.

In the generations immediately preceding and following 1914, the novel underwent a radical redefinition of its nature and possibilities. The present series of monographs is devoted to the novelists who created the modern novel and to those who, in their turn, either continued and extended, or reacted against and rejected, the traditions established during that period of intense exploration and experiment. It includes a number of those who lived and wrote in the nineteenth century but whose innovative contribution to the art of fiction makes it impossible to ignore them in any account of the origins of the modern novel; it also includes the so-called 'modernists' and those who in the mid- and late twentieth century have emerged as outstanding practitioners of this genre. The scope is, inevitably, international; not only, in the migratory and exile-haunted world of our centruy, do writers refuse to heed national frontiers – 'English' literature lays claim to Conrad the Pole, Henry James the American, and Joyce the Irishman – but geniuses such as Flaubert, Dostoevsky and Kafka have had an influence on the fiction of many nations.

Each volume in the series is intended to provide an introduction to the fiction of the writer concerned, both for those approaching him or her for the first time and for those who are already familiar with some parts of the achievement in question and now wish to place it in the context of the total *oeuvre*. Although essential information relating to the writer's life and times is given, usually in an opening chapter, the approach is primarily critical and the emphasis is not upon 'background' or generalisations but upon close examination of important texts. Where an author is notably prolific, major texts have been made to convey, more summarily, a sense of the nature and quality of the author's work as a whole. Those who want to read further will find suggestions in the select bibliography included in each volume. Many novelists are, of course, not only novelists but also poets, essayists, biographers, dramatists, travel writers and so forth; many have practised shorter forms of fiction; and many have written letters or kept diaries that constitute a significant part of their literary output. A brief study cannot hope to deal with all these in detail, but where the shorter fiction and the non-fictional writings, public and private, have an important relationship to the novels, some space has been devoted to them.

NORMAN PAGE

Chronology

1882	2 February: birth of Joyce (Rathgar, Dublin).
1886	Defeat of Gladstone's First Home Rule Bill.
1888	Joyce to Clongowes Wood College.
1890	Death of Newman.
1891	Death of Parnell.
1893	Joyce to Belvedere College.
1895	Wilde's trial and imprisonment.
1897	Queen Victoria's Diamond Jubilee.
1899	Joyce to University College, Dublin. Second Boer War.
1900	'Ibsen's New Drama'. Founding of British Labour Party.
1901	'The Day of the Rabblement'. Queen Victoria died.
1902	'James Clarence Mangan'. J's first Paris trip and reviews. Balfour's Education Act.
1903	Mary Jane Joyce (J's mother) died.
1904	Elopement with Nora to Pola (Austro-Hungary). Opening of Abbey Theatre in Dublin.
1905	Moved to Trieste. 27 July: Giorgio born.
1906	Brief residence in Rome. Samuel Beckett born.
1907	Moved back to Trieste. 26 July: Lucia born. *Chamber Music* published. 'Playboy' riots.
1909	August and October–December trips to Dublin. Letters to Nora written.
1910	H. G. Wells's *The History of Mr Polly*.
1911	Further educational and social reform in Britain.
1912	Charlie Chaplin's first film.
1914	Archduke shot in Sarajevo. First World War breaks out. Home Rule passed but shelved. *A Portrait* serialised in *The Egoist*. *Dubliners* published by Grant Richards. *Giacomo Joyce* written.
1915	J moved to Zurich. 16 June: work on *Ulysses* resumed. *Exiles* composed.
1916	*A Portrait* published in America. Easter Rising in Dublin.

1917	*A Portrait* published in Britain. Yeats's *Wild Swans at Coole.*
1918	*Ulysses* serialisation begins in *Little Review.* Conclusion of First World War. Partial franchise for women in the UK. Irish rebel Con Markiewicz elected first British woman MP. *Exiles* published.
1920	J moved to Paris. *Ulysses* serialisation halted.
1921	Irish Free State (excluding six counties) founded (December).
1922	*Ulysses* published in Paris (February).
1923	'Rory O'Conor' sketch begun (March). Brendan Behan born.
1924	First section of *Work in Progress* ('Mamalujo') published in *Transatlantic Review*, 1.
1925	G. B. Shaw awarded Nobel Prize. Yeats's *A Vision.* Eisenstein's *Battleship Potemkin.*
1926	Wall Street Crash. Baird demonstrated television picture.
1927	Book I of *Wake* (*Work in Progress*) serialised in *transition* (April–November). Cinema 'Talkies'. *Pomes Penyeach* published.
1928	Book III of *Wake* in *transition* (March–November). Full suffrage for women in the UK. Norma Jean Mortensen (Marilyn Monroe) born.
1929	*Our Exagmination* essays published.
1930	Hitler dissolved Reichstag.
1931	Joyce's residence in Kensington and marriage.
1932	De Valera's Fianna Fail took office in Ireland. Hitler became German Chancellor. Lucia diagnosed 'hebephrenic'.
1933	Leavis attacked *Work in Progress* in *Scrutiny.*
1934	Hitler became Führer.
1936	*Ulysses* published. Abdication of Edward VIII.
1937	New Irish constitution established.
1938	Beckett's *Murphy* published. *Anschluss* of Austria.
1939	J moved to Zurich. Outbreak of Second World War. *Finnegans Wake* published. Behan arrested. Seamus Heaney born. W. B. Yeats died.
1941	13 January: J died in Zurich aged 59.

Introduction

This is a book addressed to ordinary readers of fiction who may wish to begin reading Joyce, and to students and teachers who are working on Joyce's texts as a part of their study of literature. I make no apology for adding another one to the pile of critical syntheses about Joyce. The more specialist criticism that appears, the more we need such syntheses to digest, assimilate and communicate it. New readers bring new issues and new perspectives into whose terms the importance of well-known literary texts needs to be repeatedly retranslated.

In what follows I have tried to keep these readers in mind and make my critical account of Joyce's work as straightforward, broadly based, informative and accessible as it can be without being compromised or inaccurate, and without resorting to such extremes of reductiveness and common-sensicality as would disable any reader from gaining access to the highly developed and intellectually exciting world of specialist Joyce criticism and theory.

Joyce may well be the most studied, the most taught, the most read-about and the most debated of all the writers of this century. His work was challenging and modern from the very beginning, helping to shake the foundations of Victorian and Edwardian respectability and inaugurate what we understand as modernity in consciousness. Though initially neglected, condemned and abused, his works made him an idol of the radical and the avant-garde. Now that his achievements are almost universally acknowledged, they still remain problematic and unsettling, and his legacy is more often appropriated than understood. Since Yeats recognised the force of Joyce's talent at the start of the century, generations of writers have themselves had to come to terms with its power. Such writers include major contemporaries like Eliot, Lawrence and Woolf, whose greatest works can be seen to have been in part responses to their reading of Joyce. Irish writers from Beckett and O'Brien to Donleavy and Banville have all had to stand in Joyce's shadow or else to attempt to forge independent traditions to try to evade it. British writers, whether George Orwell, Dylan Thomas, Iris Murdoch, B. S. Johnson, Anthony Burgess, Martin Amis or Salman

Rushdie, have all somehow had to negotiate, whether to shun or else to embrace exultantly, the Joycean example.

Post-modern writers of fiction on the American continent (whether North Americans such as Nin and Miller in the 1930s or South Americans like Borges or Marquez), the most inventive and interesting of English language writers from the Commonwealth, and such Europeans as the writers of the French *nouveau roman* have often claimed Joyce as a principal inspiration. Contemporary poets and dramatists in America, Britain and Ireland have had Joyce no less on their minds.

Generations of literary and linguistic theorists have been forced to encounter the Joycean example and many of them have made that example central to their work. The modern study of Joyce's work enjoys the rewards of being and having been at the state of the art in computerised textual editing, in literary biography, in the international co-operations and discussions represented by increasing numbers of academic conferences, in translating, in the advances in theoretical approaches to literature that include feminism, cultural materialism, structuralism, Lacanian and other psychoanalysis and deconstruction. Such prominent theorists as Jacques Lacan, Julia Kristeva and Jacques Derrida all participated in a single Joyce conference in Frankfurt in 1984.

No single introductory (or any other) book could hope to reflect, still less contain, the whole of this still-burgeoning activity. Any approach must be partial in countless acknowledged and unacknowledged ways, just as any critical discourse, however transparently 'introductory', must betray a certain configuration of allegiances and assumptions. The present study uses many of the familiar tools of criticism: attentive reading, explication of structural pattern and detail, historical and literary contextualisation, genetic comparison, respect of stated authorial intentions, summary of interpretative possibilities and so on. Throughout, my arguments have been informed, sometimes explicitly, sometimes tacitly, by the discoveries of what I take to be the best and most up-to-date Joyce criticism. The reading I provide is also not unaffected by the recent upsurge of anti-intentionalist psychoanalytic, sociological, philosophical and linguistic theories of literature. The mixture is, I hope, not an untypical one and may serve to introduce the reader to some of the kinds of discussion they might expect to find in academic study of these texts.

I have restricted myself to a largely sequential treatment of Joyce's major novelistic works, all but neglecting his poems, including the prose-poem *Giacomo Joyce*, most of his critical writings and his play *Exiles*, which I would encourage any interested reader to explore. To some specialists, some of what follows may seem to plough over old furrows. I have for the most part, however, given new formulations of many established perceptions and not infrequently, I hope, arrived at new insights and positions.

Although it would not be in the least bit appropriate to make any elaborate declaration, definition or defence of critical stance in such a book as this, I would describe my orientation as broadly post-culturalist in its assumptions, in that it depends upon many of the assumptions about cultural context implicit in my previous work on Joyce and sexuality merged with an intensified consciousness of the hermeneutic problems said to be characteristic of the post-modern age. These assumptions are neither anti-textual, anti-historical, anti-liberal nor anti-humanistic but are nevertheless fractured and run through with a whole variety of perceptions – post-Marxist, post-formalistic, post-Barthesian, post-feministic, post-colonial, post-deconstructive and so on – that were taken to be antithetical to liberal humanism at least as it became ossified as the acceptable complacency of the human sciences in the 1950s and 1960s.

Thanks in great part to Joyce himself, literary studies have come quite a long way since the practices that drove Stephen Dedalus (himself, after all, one of the newer students of this newish discipline) to despair: 'nominal definitions, essential definitions and examples or dates of birth or death, chief works, a favourable and an unfavourable criticism side by side' (*P*, 181). A more acute sense of the historical and contextual implications of interpretation is now available to us. The chronology with which the present work begins is designed not to reduce but to enable further exploration of, for instance, the problematic delays and odd overlapping order of the publication of Joyce's major works; the booms and slumps of his compositional energies; the possible relations of his works to a variety of adducible interpretational contexts: to crises in his life, to the struggle for Irish independence, to social and technological change in Britain and on the European and world stage.

A central Joyce paradox is that the radical openness to interpretation that characterises Joyce's writings has itself caused those writings to be almost swamped with a wide range of conflicting and mutually reinforcing or debilitating rereadings that have distorted some of the urgencies and radicalisms of their initial impact. An obvious example is the way in which Joyce's lifelong Faustian and secularist struggle against the Catholic Church of his education and upbringing has become obscured by generations of interpretations that salvage biblical and liturgical resonances or patristic intellectual structures from his *oeuvre*. To subsequent generations of more secular or non-Catholic readers, Joyce may seem so deeply immersed in his Catholicism that his anger and apostasy might be ignored.

A further problem may result from the very fact of Joyce's acceptance as one of the greatest of modern writers and the apparently inevitable dilution that such acceptance entails. I have hoped to keep Joyce's radicalism, his 'offensiveness' before me where appropriate. If this means that my own reading may occasionally seem to be offensive to some others, the responsibility may not all be laid at Joyce's door. Such offences may be tolerated if not excused by the recognition that, when it comes to critical readings of Joyce, this is not the only one.

The places where my intellectual debts begin and end may be lost without trace in the countless valued contacts with other workers in the field that I have enjoyed over several years and in the generations of brilliant reading, rereading and research by an ever-increasing community of Joyce scholars that I have been privileged to encounter whether in print or in the flesh. By no means all of this can be acknowledged in detail. As a poor substitute I have made short parenthetical references in the text as an acknowledgement of debt and as an indication of possible directions for further reading. Fuller references to a selection of relevant works are appended to each chapter, though I have avoided duplicating references to works cited in more than one chapter. Each of these books and articles itself contains more substantial bibliographical information which the interested reader will, no doubt, be hungry to explore.

READING LIST

Derek Attridge (ed.), *Cambridge Companion to James Joyce* (Cambridge: Cambridge University Press, 1990).

Derek Attridge and Daniel Ferrer (eds), *Post-Structuralist Joyce* (Cambridge: Cambridge University Press, 1984).

Bernard Benstock *et al.* (ed.), *The Augmented Ninth: Proceedings of the Ninth International James Joyce Symposisum, Frankfurt 1984,* (Syracuse: Syracuse University Press, 1988).

Richard Brown, *James Joyce and Sexuality* (Cambridge: Cambridge University Press, 1985).

Richard Ellmann, *James Joyce.* rev. edn (Oxford: Oxford University Press, 1982).

Suzette Henke, *James Joyce and the Politics of Desire* (London: Routledge, 1990).

Cheryl Herr, *James Joyce's Anatomy of Culture* (Chicago: University of Illinois Press, 1986).

Colin MacCabe, *James Joyce and the Revolution of the Word* (London: Macmillan, 1978).

Dominic Manganiello, *James Joyce and Politics* (London: Routledge, 1980).

Patrick Parrinder, *James Joyce* (Cambridge: Cambridge University Press, 1984).

John-Paul Riquelme, *James Joyce: Oscillating Perspectives* (Baltimore: Johns Hopkins, 1979).

Bonnie Kime Scott, *James Joyce* (Brighton: Harvester, 1986).

William York Tindall, *A Reader's Guide to James Joyce* (New York: Noonday, 1959).

1

Dubliners

CITY OF FAILURE

The first work of Joyce's artistic maturity was published in 1914 by the prominent English publisher Grant Richards. This was a success for Joyce but one that had been long delayed since the publication of the first story in the collection (in an earlier version) in a Dublin journal called the *Irish Homestead* in 1904. The fifteen stories had taken him another three years to complete but their publication had been held up for ten years because of arguments over the sexually and politically contentious material that Joyce recorded in the speech of (and in his own implied attitude to) his Dublin people, and because of an undoubted failure on the part of successive publishers either to appreciate fully the artistic value of Joyce's stories or perhaps to risk facing the reactions that they might provoke.

Bearing these delays in mind, the stories have a remarkable consistency of character and quality and the collection has a remarkable coherence. According to Joyce's plan, the stories deal successively with protagonists or situations concerning youth, adolescence (a state that, for Joyce, continued until the 'thirty-four or thirty-five' of Bob Doran), maturity and public life. Representing varieties of that narrow-minded Edwardian bourgeois dullness, which Joyce called 'paralysis', the characters include the unnamed, innocent small boy of the first three stories. There are provincials like Jimmy Doyle, who gets out of his depth in fast company, in 'After the Race'; Little Chandler, who is an envious foil to the successful journalist Gallagher in 'A Little Cloud'; and the clerk Farrington for whom drink is no real escape from the failures of a lowly working life in 'Counterparts'. The shabby and, as we would now say, sexist 'Two

Gallants', Corley and Lenehan, are, no less than the paedophiliac
pervert in 'An Encounter' and the ubiquitous celibates, offered as
symptoms of a pervasively rotten Dublin sexuality. The maudlin
anecdotalists O'Connor, Henchy, Hynes and Crofton in 'Ivy Day in
the Committee Room' stand for an emasculated politics. Joyce's
Dubliners are not, of course, all men: they include the girl in
'Eveline', whose terrifying inertia in response to the elopement plans
of her (albeit potentially deceitful) suitor Frank is surely one of the
clearest examples of what Joyce meant by 'paralysis' in these people.
There are monstrously domineering mothers in Mrs Mooney in 'A
Boarding House' and Mrs Kearney in 'A Mother', and the painfully
and dependently chaste Maria in 'Clay'. James Duffy in 'A Painful
Case' and Gabriel Conroy in 'The Dead' (whom Torchiana, 1986, sees
as the little boy grown up) seem clogged by their own (at least partly
failed) literary ambitions. Some characters are cursed by religion,
others by drink. Kernan in 'Grace' suffers from a very serious
overdose of both.

The themes of the stories include the deadening influence of
bourgeois social conformity, the stranglehold of the Catholic Church
and the impotence of a Dublin that suffered, at that time, under the
increasingly unwelcome pressures of British rule. On returning to
Dublin in August 1909 Joyce let loose his private frustrations at the
city that was for him 'the city of failure, of rancour and of
unhappiness' (*SL*, 163) and in his stories he subtly interrogates and
exposes an ugly social brew of enforced chastity, suppressed
prostitution, hypocrisy, ignorance and exploitation that made up
society of the time.

The irony and ambiguity of Joyce's writing and its austere refusal to
force a judgement upon a reader has been widely recognised to be at
the centre of its importance (Kenner, 1956). Such austerity might be
seen as a Swiftian aloofness or disdain, but interpretative licence may
be given to the reader in the context of a more Blakean libertarian
social vision. The stories lend themselves to be read in terms of the
social Freudianism identifiable with more recent thinkers of the
Freudian left such as Herbert Marcuse and Norman O. Brown. The
stories contemptuously detail all kinds of social constraint or
inhibition and, at a time of great external political upheaval, attempt to
mount a parallel upheaval of interior mental life. Unlike Blake, the
stories are remarkable for the perfectionist fidelity with which they

re-create character, locality, social circumstance and idiom. Yet to call Joyce only a 'realist' writer with certain moral themes and attitudes is to miss the intensity, anger and virtuosity of his genius.

Typically, in forming a vocabulary to explain his writing, Joyce drew on the language of the Catholic ritual he rejected so strongly. The *Dubliners* stories he described as *epicleti*, apparently meaning that they were to be thought of as moments of transformation analogous to the transformation of bread and wine in the Catholic Mass. The term is like the much better-known one 'epiphany', which Joyce used as the term for his first creative prose, poetic and dramatic fragments that he composed, and subsequently theorised in his first attempt at sustained fictional self-portraiture *Stephen Hero*. There the 'epiphany' is defined as a 'sudden spiritual manifestation' or 'showing forth' and many readers have used the term as a way of seeing Joyce's stories as a kind of spiritual 'eureka' where the characters suddenly and guiltily discover a previously unsuspected truth about their own inadequacy (Magalaner, 1959).

In certain stories this does indeed seem to happen: the boy in 'An Encounter' ends up 'penitent', the one in 'Araby' sees himself as 'a creature driven and derided by vanity'. There is a danger, though, of reducing the stories to a morality of self-imposed guilt and constraint, which was precisely the one that Joyce set out to escape and to oppose. Such final guilty recognitions as these characters may be said to experience should surely be read as other symptoms of, rather than as intuitions of escape from, their 'moral paralysis'. Alongside Jimmy Doyle's recognition of his 'folly' at losing at cards and Chandler's 'tears of remorse' at failing to comfort his child should be posed the endings of stories like 'Counterparts' where there is no recogniton of guilt, like 'Eveline' where the recognition is even more intensely that there is no recognition, or like 'Grace' where a remorseful attitude seems to be deliberately mocked.

The theorising of the Stephen in Joyce's early autobiographical novel *Stephen Hero* can help us here, since he argues that anything can have an 'epiphany', even the clock on Dublin's Ballast Office. Not all readers have always been aware of the radicalism, from Joyce's point of view, of hijacking these terms and using them for antithetical secular ends, or of the radicalism of Joyce's desire to include the ordinary or the apparently insignificant within artistic forms that seemed – and often still seem – to be intrinsically prejudiced in favour of the genteel social context or the Yeatsian/Jungian kind of symbol whose significance has already been loaded full.

In this as in other respects the social class of Joyce's Dubliners is extremely important (Parrinder, 1986). They are not quite the proletarians that were just beginning to enter English fiction in the 1890s: neither the sentimentalised proletarian realism of Arthur Morrison's *Tales of Mean Streets*, George Moore's *Esther Waters* or Kipling nor the radical proletarianism of Robert Tressell's *Ragged Trousered Philanthropists* (a novel that may well have been on Richards's desk around the same time as *Dubliners* and also suffered cutting before it got into print). Neither are they quite the lower-middle class shopkeepers like Lewisham, Mr Polly or Kipps that were currently in vogue in the fictions of H. G. Wells. They are neither the idealised peasantries nor the leisured ascendancy class typical of nineteenth-century Irish fiction nor the war-torn urban proletariat of O'Casey's Dublin.

Joyce's discovery was a subtler mixture than any of these. His characters are 'low' enough to shock the genteel and to seem 'realistic' rather than idealised to the largely middle-class mass audience for fiction that was just beginning to be opened more widely by the educational reforms of Victorian and Edwardian liberalism. They cannot be patronised. Their failures and inadequacies are too close to those of their readership. Yet they are, for the most part, startingly limited and mean, trapped within the narrow confines of their limited ideas, limited both in their senses of respectability and of freedom. Lacking a true sense of enterprise, their only ways of escaping their lot seem to be despairing drunkenness, cynical exploitation, superficial self-promotion or flight into exile.

In portraying them in this way, Joyce may be said to create a shattering and dynamic self-division on the part of his reader, who is forced into recognising an identity with these characters and at the same time forced to recognise the utter bankruptcy of their existence. In such ways Joyce's stories re-enact the tensions of a social world that was in 1914 in the process of rapid change, even collapse, on a European scale and has, in some ways, been repeating similar tensions and collapses ever since.

In Ireland, breaking away from the British Empire in the years immediately before and after the European-wide upheavals of the First World War, Joyce felt strong pressures of ideology, old and new. In this profound sense, as in the more obvious senses of their fidelity to locality (much interpreted by Torchiana), Joyce's stories are importantly Irish, but they are also very British or even English in their austerity and reserve, and they are uncompromisingly international in their relevance to us today.

Joyce's politics were radical and important enough to drive him into nomadic exile. They encompassed almost every aspect of his personal life, the experiences of the characters in his fictions, the narrative forms of those fictions, and pervaded every aspect of his literary styles and techniques. They are so important that they were almost entirely missed by the first generation of critics of his work. Few would say that these politics manifest themselves simply in terms of nationality, or of the struggle to represent social class. Questions of personal rather than public life predominate (though it might be noted that these terms were not always starkly opposed in the Dublin of the turn of the century, and that Joyce's work anticipates the further erosion of that opposition in our time).

Joyce's politics emerged in literary language, most especially as a decisive move away from the idea of the author as someone with only one 'style', however ironic, and towards greater experiment in the manipulation of existing literary styles and techniques and the discovery of a range of new ones. Perhaps, in these stories, his politics emerged most of all in the first of Stephen Daedalus's three central watchwords – 'silence, exile and cunning' – in silence.

THE SILENCE OF 'THE SISTERS'

To talk of the silences of these stories is not just to use a critical metaphor. They can be seen from the start in the text of the first story in the collection, 'The Sisters', and can provide the key to a first reading of the stories (Rabaté, 1991).

To begin at the beginning, the story meticulously tracks the responses of a sensitive, possibly orphaned, boy to the death of a local parish priest James Flynn, whom he has known and who has apparently befriended him. The boy lives with his aunt and his uncle Jack and the only other characters who appear are the uncle's friend, a distiller called Old Cotter, and the two sisters of the title, Nannie and Eliza, who tend to the priest's corpse. They are Flynn's sisters in the literal sense, but just as important is the atmosphere of sorority that pervades the story. As in the opening section of Joseph Conrad's story *Heart of Darkness*, this partly depends on echoes of the three Fates of classical mythology or the Norns of Wagnerian Nordicism.

Yet Joyce's eye for locality and social circumstance weighs as heavily as mythic allusion here. The fact that these are sisters speaks implicitly of the priest's vows of celibacy and of the institutions of female celibacy that characterised Irish society of the time. Readers of *Ulysses* would do well to compare these sisters with the pair of 'Dublin vestals' whose paralysis and conformism Stephen's satire immolates in 'The Parable of the Plums' which he tells in the newspaper office episode.

Incest is not mentioned in the story, but the claustrophobic, endogamous or inbred atmosphere broods menace. As in the plays of Ibsen, the story offers a close urban interior – one that may have been especially surprising to the first readers of the story in the *Irish Homestead* who read it tucked in amongst the advertisements for agricultural machinery that speak of a still largely agrarian economy. Joyce's version of what an Edwardian Irish 'homestead' *really* was leaves us still shuddering to this day. The boy's aunt notes that there was something 'uncanny' about the priest, a term whose layerings of conscious and unconscious meaning (in German the word *unheimlich* seems to contain the familiar, homely and well-known alongside the strange, menacing and repressed) were unpacked by Sigmund Freud in his essay 'The "Uncanny"' (1919) and seem especially relevant to this story.

Joyce entitled his story 'The Sisters' but most readers have found the centre of its interest in the fascinating sensibility of the friendless, unparented, inquisitive little boy, who narrates and refracts the story through his own naïve perceptions. He is far more in 'exile' from the world around him than such literal exiles in the stories as Ignatius Gallaher in 'A Little Cloud'. For him the social world is a puzzling array of opaque or transparent signs that he struggles to decode or else records in their opaque form.

Perhaps it is this very incomprehension that makes him so particularly interested in language itself. Whereas his thoughts and memories are obviously coloured and limited by his own perception (for instance the dream he has, which he can only record in an incomplete and unexplained fragment), the dialogue of the adults around him is given with the accuracy of a tape-recorder. Old Cotter begins 'No, I wouldn't say he was exactly . . . but there was something queer . . .' This speech is also strikingly incomplete, full of elisions, hesitations and repressions marked by the recurring typographic feature of three dots. Three dots can make a triangle, and the triangle, as we later learn from *Finnegans Wake*, can stand as the elemental symbol for a space, a delta: the organ that defines the essential permeability or femininity of a text that the boy's and the reader's curiosity is invited to penetrate and repenetrate in order to fill or complete these gaps with a significance that the text may ultimately encompass or resist. We see the frustrations of the boy as he records 'I puzzled my head to extract meaning from his unfinished sentences.'

Whereas the boy is present during the conversations of the adults, he says remarkably little. More typically he suppresses his speech, saying 'I crammed my mouth with stirabout' (the Anglo-Irish word for porridge subtly evoking a non-verbal confusedness). Characters repeatedly hesitate or fail to speak, or else they murmur or mumble. The boy will not even eat cream-crackers in case he makes too much noise eating them. Towards the end 'silence took possession of the little room'.

The adults seem to communicate according to a language in which everybody already knows everything and nothing needs to be said outright. The boy's two questions are particularly telling in this respect. Firstly, in asking 'Who?', he is shown demanding a name in a story where names are very sparingly used, his own not given at all. Secondly, in asking 'Is he dead?', he breaks the code of secrecy and silence that dominates elsewhere. 'Did he . . . peacefully?' is his aunt's version of this unaskable question. The adults prefer to leave great mysteries of love and death unspoken, while the child wishes to hear them spelled out in simple words. Of course there may be specific mysteries concealed beneath these silences but we can be confident that we will never know their identity.

The boy's thoughts (which he confides to the reader if not to the adults in the story) also dwell on language. There is the secret language of the window which he tries to read: if he can see candlelight inside, the priest will have died, otherwise not. He notes the special language of the distillery, the 'faints' and 'worms' that once fascinated him in the talk of Old Cotter. Signs echo in his consciousness: the sign in the drapery shop 'Umbrellas Re-covered' and the memorial notice announcing the priest's death.

He is struck by the language of the priest's two sisters with its telling errors: Eliza who mistakes 'rheumatic' for pneumatic tyres; and Nannie who tumbles unwittingly into a paradoxical admission of her own inevitable subservience to authority by referring to *The Freeman's Journal* as the *Freeman's General*. The sisters' mala-propisms show them to be the uneasy users of a language that many Irish people have felt to be a living memory of the impositions of English colonialism. But all kinds of authority and imposition effected through language seem to be relevant. In the language of the ritual of the Catholic Church a still more ancient imperialism is remembered, imposing another kind of foreignness upon the boy that he had experienced when, as he records, the priest 'taught me to pronounce Latin properly'.

The priest has attempted to explain the rituals of the Church to the boy who tried to memorise the responses of the Mass but he stumbled or, as he puts it 'pattered'. It is a word that can mean to hesitate or to jumble one's speech, though more usually in modern English serves to describe a kind of sales-talk or jargon (Old Cotter's special language of the distillery is one kind of 'patter'). Joyce's choice of the word here, though, takes us right back to its original meaning, in the recitation of what were at that time the foreign-language rituals and prayers or 'Paternosters' of the Catholic Church.

Joyce's two versions of the story might instructively be compared. In the earlier version the sisters themselves are described more fully and an attitude to them more explicitly offered. The boy's narration includes a present-tense element that is omitted in the more mysterious and more distanced later version. The dialogue is sharpened; details, such as the boy's dream and his failed attempt to pray, are added. The chalice is made more important and the repeated description of the priest's face as 'truculent' introduced. Both the beginning and ending are changed.

The first version begins in this way:

Three nights in succession I had found myself in Great Britain-street at that hour, as if by Providence. Three nights also I had raised my eyes to that lighted square of window and speculated. I seemed to understand that it would occur at night. But in spite of the Providence that had led my feet, and in spite of the reverent curiosity of my eyes, I had discovered nothing. Each night the square was lighted in the same way, faintly and evenly. It was not the light of candles so far as I could see. Therefore it had not yet occurred. (*Irish Homestead*, August 1904)

The final version is expanded. The boy's three visits have become the priest's three strokes. The prospect of 'no hope' that some readers have thought of as a subtle allusion to Dante's *Inferno* is added. Any role of 'Providence' is obscured. The interesting reference to Great Britain Street, which seems to suggest that Joyce thought of the story as a kind of Arthur Morrison microcosm for any street in Britain, is deferred until its second mention later in the story. (The real street in Dublin, where Joyce was later to set the 'Cyclops' bar-room episode of *Ulysses*, is called Little Britain Street: Torchiana, 1986.)

The idea of the lighted window is clarified but most of all those three terms that so puzzle the boy are put into the forefront of the reader's mind. The paraylsis (or 'hemiplegia' of the will as Joyce glossed it in a letter) kills the priest but not until he has infected the whole of Dublin society with a dose of it. To bullish Joyce critics (who sometimes seem to suffer from the opposite complaint, a kind of hypertrophy of the will to interpret) the other two terms 'gnomon' and 'simony' have offered no less of a red rag.

A gnomon, according to the *OED*, can be the pointer in a sundial, or a carpenter's square, or, in geometry, the figure that remains from a parallelogram when a similar parallelogram has been removed from one of its corners: a distorted thick 'L' shape in other words. More obscurely, the term may mean any odd number. Is Joyce placing an irresolvably obscure puzzle in the boy's mind here, or does the word have some hidden importance for the boy or for the story as a whole? Traditional interpreters would pursue the latter course, arguing perhaps, that the boy is thinking of the priest, who, after his stroke, may be an empty shape of what he was before or perhaps a 'pointer' or 'indicator' of some kind. A critic working in a deconstructive tradition may prefer not to interpret, arguing that an irreducible puzzle would itself be important to the story, alerting us to the puzzles and absurdities of mental life and the necessary opacity of all linguistic signs.

'Simony' (or the selling of spiritual favours) is also puzzling, but easier, at least, to apply to the priest, since when he appears to the boy in a dream, it is as a 'simonaic' that he is described, begging to be absolved of his sins. Some kind of guilt at the implications of the Church's purported transcendance over the commercial seems to be the point.

What is the secret of the paralytic priest that the story so maddeningly incites us to pursue? How should we explain his 'truculent' manner in death or the incident when he was found laughing in his confession box? What is the significance of the incident of the dropped chalice that seems to be the first symptom of his incipient disease? Is his 'paralysis', as Florence Walzl has argued, the 'general paralysis of the insane' resulting from hereditary or acquired syphilis about which Joyce's medical students often joke? Or is he, like so many other characters in the stories, paralytic with alcoholic drink? Does he conceal a guilty sin of incest with his sisters, or of pederastic longing for the boy? Has he gone mad because, as the sisters say, he was 'too scrupulous' or, as the boy suspects in the earlier version, in despair at the contrast between his 'old life' of study in Rome and the lack of intelligence in his contemporary surroundings.

Any or all of these explanations are possible but none are conclusive, and most critics might be most satisfied to think of the priest's enigmatic 'truculence' as an image of enigma itself, his failed Mass a terrifying confrontation with the hollowness of the symbols with which he holds sway over his flock, the atmosphere of secrecy and surveillance, the repeated silences of the tale barely concealing the inevitability of death and the failed transcendences of ritual.

A despairing intimation of the inefficacy of the ritual and its collapse into hypocrisy and cliché seems indicated in the ending of the original version, with the description of the priest found laughing to himself and the revealingly flat phrase 'Then they knew that something was wrong' followed by the clichéd supplication 'God rest his soul'. In the final version the despairing intimation is there in the final image of the priest lying in his coffin, 'an idle chalice on his breast'. But then the dialogue resumes with Eliza's repetition of the story of the priest's telling laughter and with the blank phrase 'there was something gone wrong with him . . .' ending with an incompletion, with three further dots that seem to indicate an emptiness that goes even beyond despair. The mysterious death of the Father has given birth to the author in Joyce.

BEYOND THE PLEASURE PRINCIPLE

Sexual psychopathology bred by silence and repression breathes an odour of corruption on the stories from which neither childhood nor adolescence (running well into middle age) is exempt. Joyce's second story follows two boys on a day's adventure that is soured by 'An Encounter' with a paedophile who talks 'mysteriously' to them about girls and about the 'nice warm whipping' of boys in the classroom that he 'would love . . . better than anything in this world' (*D*, 27–8). From the perspective of the boy's innocence the exact nature of what is going on is unclear and silence works overtime in the reader's imagination:

> After a silence of a few minutes I heard Mahoney exclaim:
> – I say! Look what he's doing!
> As I neither answered nor raised my eyes Mahoney exclaimed again:
> – I say he's a queer old josser!   (*D*, 26)

The silence implies an experienced and attentive reader though Joyce ended up having to point out to his publisher the irony that the printers who had objected to swear words elsewhere in the text apparently failed even to note what was taking place (*SL*, 83). The idea that the boy's final 'penitence' (Tindall, 1959) or the political implications of the story's topography (Torchiana, 1986) account for its meaning seem to compound silence with evasion. A still more disturbing strain may underpin the boys' attitude, which, at least in the case of Mahoney and his idea of switching names, seems to mix caution with an element of teasing.

The ageing adolescent Corley boasts of his seduction of a servant girl to his grisly accomplice Lenehan. But there is no more romance in their 'encounter' since Corley evidently sees her mainly to get her to steal from her employer so that he can go out and drink. The men callously exploit the women but women (like the Mrs Mooney who traps her innocent if thirty-five-year-old lodger into marrying her daughter) can be predators too.

'Eveline', the second story Joyce had printed in the *Irish Homestead* but the fourth in the final order, was much less revised than 'The Sisters'. It is the shortest and in some ways also the most intense of the stories and one that is close in spirit to 'The Parable of the Plums' that Stephen extemporises as a parody of Joyce's stories in the 'Aeolus' episode of *Ulysses*. It is one of the three stories in the collection that has a female central character, though Joyce does not attempt to adopt the female first person for his narrative stance. Indeed Eveline herself never speaks. Above all it is the story that seems to capture the stagnant, hopeless quality of the collection most intensely as Eveline muses over her miserable life and is shown in a devastating act of failure to elope with her mysterious lover Frank as he sails for 'Buenos Ayres'.

This stagnation is most starkly voiced through the potent device of repetition. The first and longest part of the story is an evening reverie that begins with her head 'leaning against the window curtains' and the 'odour of dusty cretonne' and ends with a nearly exact repetition of the phrase. Such repetition is by no means unique in fiction and Joyce may well have been remembering the similar repetition of an opening phrase in George Moore's highly popular novel *Esther Waters* (1894).

Repetition is a key element in musical and indeed all artistic form, but such jarringly exact repetition as this strikes the reader as disturbing. Freudian theory of such compulsive repetition is surely relevant here. It upset Freud's early belief that psychology was to be explained in terms of twin nutritive and sexual hungers and seemed to expose dark, death-seeking motivations, which he began to explore in *Beyond the Pleasure Principle*. Eveline is not unlike most of Joyce's Dubliners in that she has suppressed her libidinous desires almost entirely in favour of a paralysing, compulsive round of self-torturing despair, and this story is as much as anything an account of that.

Frequent studies of the language of the story have shown how Joyce creates this atmosphere. Everything moves around Eveline. The evening (with which her name sets up an echo) 'invades' the avenue, and in its later description as 'deepening' seems more active than she. She merely 'leans' or 'is' or 'continues' to be. Towards the end of the story there is a moment of hope for decisive, liberating action when she 'stood up in a sudden impulse of terror' but even that verb becomes a terrible pun when in the final scene of the story we are told that she not only 'stood' but 'gripped' and 'clutched' at the iron railing and her actions become more and more negative and inert.

Echoes of other repetitions in the world of the stories are triggered in Eveline's thoughts. The child-beating and drunkenness of her father who is 'usually fairly bad on Saturday night' and leaves all the housekeeping and housework to her, anticipates the figure of Farrington in 'Counterparts'. Marriage may, of course, offer no escape but another repetition of entrapment, as this little conundrum of her thoughts ironically seems to imply: 'Then she would be married – she Eveline. People would treat her with respect then. She would not be treated as her mother had been.' The cycles of marital entrapment in 'A Boarding House' are clearly anticipated here. The usual array of ghosts – a dead mother; a dead brother and the yellowing photograph of a priest who has left for Australia – haunt her imagination. The invasions of red-brick suburbia and brown-baggaged soldiers on the quayside ghost wider social and political constraints.

Repeated dichotomies between home and away, between the routine and the exotic, between staying with the familiar and escaping to the adventurous underpin the story and cause a further scrics of repetitions. A life of 'commonplace sacrifices closing in final craziness' is set against exciting 'tales of distant countries'. Frank takes her to see a popular light opera, *The Bohemian Girl*, and they even sit in 'an unfamiliar part of the theatre'. Joyce felt profoundly what the poet Philip Larkin calls 'The Importance of Elsewhere'; unlike Larkin or Eveline he decided to take off and go. The story interestingly poses Eveline in a state of balance, typically leaving the reader with the Brechtian decision-making task. Following the chain of associations gathering around the word 'home' offers a potential justification for her staying. 'Home' is after all precisely what Frank is offering her and who knows whether that home will be any better than her present one? Perhaps we can say too that her decision to opt for 'escape' may lead her to escape from her father but also leaves her with the possibility she ultimately seems to take: of escaping from Frank. Several readers have found Frank an implausible and probably deceitful figure but a contrast with the home-accepting, flight-denying poems of Larkin may help to put such readings into perspective.

The last words of the story leave Eveline in a deliberately ambiguous state, illegible to Frank and to the reader: 'Her eyes gave him no sign of love, or farewell, or recognition.' This may be the ultimate kind of paralysis just as it is the ultimate kind of silence which goes far beyond the mere failure to speak. Perhaps this sign, which is 'no sign', echoes Eveline's mother's last mad words, 'Derevaun Seraun! Derevaun Seraun!', a phrase first thought to be Irish Gaelic (Tindall, 1959) but which has resisted such easy translation or explanation, to the extent that some recent critics (McCormack, 1983) argue that its very incomprehensibility in a context of cultural and linguistic exclusion is explanation enough.

DOUBLES AND 'COUNTERPARTS'

'Counterparts', the ninth of the fifteen stories, paints one of the most damning pictures of Dublin life and has one of the least apparently sympathetic central characters. It opens in a place of work, the office of Crosbie & Alleyne, where the clerk Farrington is suffering the sharp censure of his superior for laziness. Instead of completing the job in hand Farrington cannot resist slipping out to a nearby bar and, on returning, compounds his problems by offering a cheeky reponse to his employer's question: 'Do you take me for an utter fool?'

Like many of Joyce's Dubliners he is happiest in a bar, where alcohol and informality feed his fractured self-esteem. Such happiness is only the most fleeting escape for him, though, and is achieved at great cost: in the final scene he returns to a far from happy home where he takes out his frustrations by beating his 'whimpering' little boy.

The fact that Joyce's own father briefly held an unsuccesful clerkship in Henry Alleyne's Chapelizod Distillery Company adds a powerful autobiographical or psychosexual reading in which Joyce himself figures as victim (Restuccia, 1990). But the structure of feeling offered by the language of the story is more complex than any simple identification between author and character would allow. Both narrative method and the place of the story in the structure of maturation encourage us to see through Farrington's eyes rather than the little boy's or from any more detached moralistic or analytical perspective, and we are likely to emerge from the story with a strong sense of the conflict between narrow social constraints and the impulse to escape that promotes this unproductive and potentially destructive doubling or division in Farrington's mind.

Doublings and divisions are not only internal to Farrington. We do not get past the first page of *Finnegans Wake* before we come upon the vital pun on 'doublin' that provides whatever clue we may need to find throughout a collection of stories called *Dubliners* any number of dopplegängers or counterparts: that is characters who seem to echo, mirror or contrast each other in feature or in situation. The perception of such doublings offers us an insight into the structures of Joyce's thinking that his denial of a judging authorial or narratorial perspective may initially obscure.

There are pointed similarities between the two strongest and most autobiographical characters in the collection (James Duffy of 'A Painful Case' and Gabriel Conroy in 'The Dead') whose self-enclosed and rather pompous literarinesses are mutually illuminating and suggest two intellectual models Joyce struggled to avoid. In 'A Boarding House' Mrs Mooney's determination to get her daughter as unhappily married as she was herself prepares us for Mrs Kearney's ugly insistence on her daughter's fee in 'A Mother'. Eveline's paralysed emptiness in 'Eveline' anticipates Maria's feeble naïvety in 'Clay'. The voluble Old Cotter in 'The Sisters' foreshadows the fireside figure of Old Jack in 'Ivy Day'. The little boy persona is the same but also different in each of the first three stories. The romantic longings of the boy in 'Araby' tie him in different ways to Eveline, to Emily Sinico in 'A Painful Case' or to Gretta Conroy, whose folly is perhaps more tolerantly handled than that of any other character in the collection. Gretta's idealised absent lover Michael Furey contrasts with any one of the actual sexual misfits in the stories, though because of his absence, this love also has the flavour of pathos rather than that of triumphant erotic rapture.

In some of the stories the internal contrast between two 'counterparts' is crucial, most obviously in 'A Little Cloud' where the provincial domestic constraints of Little Chandler clearly contrast with the metropolitan adventures of Ignatius Gallaher. The 'too excited' Jimmy Doyle and his ultimate sense of his own 'folly' contrast with the apparently easy success of the racing driver Ségouin. In 'Two

Gallants' the 'base betrayer' Corley is shown in an unflattering connection with Lenehan the 'leech'.

For any or all of these stories the title 'Counterparts' would be quite appropriate and so we may ask how it applies to this story of the clerk Farrington and his frustrations at home and at work. Besides the obvious point that his job is making legal copies or 'counterparts', it is the double 'counterpart' relationships of victimiser and victim, of Mr Alleyne over Farrington and then of Farrington over his child that provide a clear thread of narrative structure and action. But then, perhaps, Farrington, with his tedious and emasculating clerkship has a 'counterpart' in Weathers, who, as theatre strong-man and acrobat, enjoys a superficially freer life. In this we might of course say that Farrington is a 'counterpart' of Little Chandler or Bob Doran, or that, in failing to escape, he contrasts or 'counterparts' Joyce himself, the one Dubliner who got away and whose triumphant flight may provide the crucial implicit contrast with all the paralysed characters in the stories. All of these versions imply a story whose central theme is a social constraint or failure of social mobility and the title may punningly emphasise this, since to be socially mobile in the Edwardian era of office clerks and shop assistants was to be known as a 'counter jumper'.

Yet the female characters are also important in the story, as are what the correspondences and contrasts between their situations might imply. Besides the 'piercing' secretary Miss Parker, there is the perfumed, rich client, the Jewish Miss Delacour, who holds the rapt attention of the boss Mr Alleyne in the first part of the story and who exudes confidence in her own sensuality. Then there is the showgirl with whom Farrington exchanges suggestive glances in the back bar of Mulligan's in Poolbeg Street. The version of this scene that Grant Richards eventually printed is toned down from the blunter version that Joyce first submitted to him. Farrington's comment that 'he wouldn't mind having the far one' and the description of the girl as she 'changed the position of her legs often' have been excised (*JJA*, 4, 85). It is 'want of money' that, ostensibly at least, prevents Farrington from following up the flirtation, and the implication, in terms of the subtle sexual codes and body-language of the time, is that the girl is a prostitute or at least that Farrington believes her to be one. Finally we have an economically painted glimpse of Farrington's wife, 'a little sharp-faced woman', who is out at the chapel when he returns and whose situation (she has five children as well as this feeble husband) has clearly made her unhappy. In this reading of the story there are four female 'counterparts' offering a bitter and incisive portrayal of restricted, mutually excluding and mutually supporting female roles: office girl, woman of means, whore and unhappy mother. To take a different reading of the punning potential of the title, these could be four ways in which women in the constrained society of the time may have been forced to trade their 'parts' across the 'counter'. The situation is one whose inner psychology and dynamic may be further explored in the terrified boy's pathetic final offer to say a 'Hail Mary' for his father. Such an appeal in such a story can only invite a reader to explore further the role of the mysterious symbol of virgin mother in the social organisation of sexual life in this self-destructively virtuous society.

Joyce's theory of character, both within the story and within the volume as a whole, plays with resemblances and alternatives in such a way that identities seem less stable than the forces that condition them, and in this way the nature of his social anger is laid bare.

THE DARK GAUNT HOUSE

There is subtle but unmistakeable Gothic potential in the description of the 'wheezy hall-door bell' and the 'dark, gaunt house on Usher's Island' that opens the final story, 'The Dead'. It seems almost a discordant note in a volume of such apparently 'realistic' stories and chance may indeed have intervened to cut it out, since in a surviving typescript the word 'gaunt' was suggestively misread as 'parent', though the mistake was spotted and corrected before the story reached print (*JJA*, 4, 506). Yet any innocent reader of a story entitled 'The Dead' might expect some Gothic excitements, whose presence may confirm the uncanny or menacing feeling that I described as being characteristic of 'The Sisters', the opening story in the volume. Both stories flirt with the Gothic convention of a ghostly revenant, yet both seem more 'realistic' or 'psychological' than the familiar fantastic tale.

Alert contemporary readers could have been reminded of the similar strategy of Ibsen's play *Ghosts*, where the ghosts of the title have little or nothing to do with the popular superstitions that underpin the usual 'ghost story' but represent the menacing sexual secrets that may be concealed beneath a veneer of middle-class respectablity and the all-too-real, physiological return from the dead of hereditary venereal disease. It took Freud until the 1920s to spell out his theory that 'uncanny' feelings in literature might best be understood in relation to repressed psychosexual material, and it is known that Ibsen's play probably helped him toward this realisation. In 1932 Joyce wrote a parodic 'Epilogue to Ibsen's *Ghosts*' which brings a comic ghost of Captain Alving back to life to justify his own excesses (and to accuse everyone else in sight of worse) and shows that Joyce too thought of ghosts as a metaphorical surfacing of what has been repressed (*CW*, 271–3). The Gothicism and social-Freudianism of these stories suggests that he was aware of this all along.

That something is uneasy in the 'dark, gaunt house' should strike any reader and that was probably enough for Joyce's purposes. As the experience of seeing the recent John Houston film of 'The Dead' makes clear, the story is set in a confined interior space throughout the three sections of its action, and this makes a sharp contrast with the free and imaginative ranging across Irish geography and from past to present and future in the mental space of the famous coda that ends the story.

Homeliness, familiarity and a precarious respectability characterise the opening section of the story in a suggestive conjuncture with this hint of menace. Some critics have noted the cheerfully innocent and colloquial idiom of the narration: the maid 'literally run off her feet', her 'scamper' to the door, the dance which was always 'a great affair' which had never 'fallen flat', and the aunts who would not take 'back answers'. Hugh Kenner (1978 p. 15) suggests that this is the idiom we might imagine being spoken by the maid Lilly herself, were she to be writing the story. Her welcoming duties create the opening atmosphere of the story but may also suggest a confinement within her terms of reference.

Does this colloquial touch echo a tradition beginning with the drunken porter in *Macbeth*? Does perhaps a Christmas-time story in which a character called 'Gabriel' makes a dramatic entrance to a 'maid' called 'Lilly' remind us of the Annunciation? If so, is it a liturgical nostalgia or a structuring undercurrent of Christian symbolism that informs the memory, or is it a more ambiguous annunciation like those of Yeats that we should see here? Or should we rather remember that Gabriel Conroy was the hero of and gave his name to the title of a popular novel by the American novelist Bret Harte which begins with a lyrical description of snow falling? Intertextual resonances are ubiquitous as ever in Joyce but equally they are well embedded in a convincing dramatic scene.

This scene serves to identify subtly Gabriel's rather awkward or distanced position at the party as he finds himself 'discomposed' by Lilly's sharp comment that 'The men that is now is only all palaver and what they can get out of you.' He reveals himself as a 'standing joke' in insisting that his wife, Gretta, wear goloshes and he worries that his superior education will make him seem a snob. Set against his arrival in this first section are the efforts of the genial Mr Browne to add some humourous and flirtatious party atmosphere and the arrival of the far more awkward but drunkenly oblivious Freddy Malins.

Part of the brilliance of the story consists in the way in which Joyce is able to capture the nervousnesses and embarrassments that often serve to make parties less than the highest expectations that their guests may have of them. Gabriel's self-conscious and sensitive personality (the narrator describes his spectacles and his 'delicate and restless eyes') may not be unequivocally positive but is the right medium with which to capture of such feelings. The second section of the story throws him into the dancing where he meets his second 'discomposure' at the hands of the 'frank-mannered, talkative' Miss Ivors. Not untypical of the Dublin of the time (which threw up female political martyrs like Constance Markiewicz, who was the first woman elected to the British Parliament, though she could not take her seat because she was imprisoned after the 1916 rising) Molly Ivors is a public woman whose nationalism and feminism give her a confidence and independence that might have seemed new and threatening, at least in the first decade of this century in Dublin.

Unlike Yeats who explored the tragic potential of such 'terrible beauty', Joyce subtly explores the mixture of old-fashioned gentlemanliness and subtle resentment that characterises Gabriel's response to Molly Ivors. The logic of Gabriel's embarrassment is complex here, as in the encounter with Lilly. Why should he feel any force in Lilly's rebuff? He, after all, seems less interested in 'palaver' than almost anyone else at the party, perhaps seeming culpably aloof. In Molly Ivors he senses a kind of hostility in her political teasing and in her very dress and manner, and he turns down her invitation to a trip to the west of Ireland since it represents to him an attachment to the narrowly national, rather than to the cosmopolitan ideal to which he aspires.

Gabriel tries to articulate an inoffensive personal, private position in relation to her public view but he is doomed to failure and to be misunderstood. Even his silence is aggressively appropriated by her for her own ends: 'Of course, you've no answer', she chides. Typically, he retreats to the company of Gretta (who inadvertently sides with Molly Ivors against him), then to Freddy Malins's mother and thence further into the 'embrasure' of the window where we are shown his thoughts in which internalised private resentment is converted into the public discourse of his after-dinner speech.

Gabriel's flight and disappearance from the public world of the party brings other characters into the forefront, notably Aunt Julia, who sings a touchingly self-revealing song for a spinster (echoing that of Maria in 'Clay'): 'Arrayed for the Bridal'. Gabriel's eyes have already strayed to the margins of the significant and have spotted the the print of the balcony scene in *Romeo and Juliet* on the unmarried womens' wall. He interprets it in terms of his aunts' education in hackneyed literary themes and embroidery. We may notice, though, that the sisters have been repeatedly shown in a posture of expectation, 'at the banisters' or 'craning her neck over the banisters', and that somewhere between Juliet and 'Aunt Julia' or between that famous balcony and these suburban banisters a latent truth about party-going resides.

For all his centrality, the story may not entirely be Gabriel's story and the other party-goers – genial Browne, who like Shakespeare's John of Gaunt can play nicely with his own name but keeps referring to Freddy Malins as Teddy; the romantic tenor Bartell D'Arcy who turns the talk to the nostalgic discussion of singers; Aunt Julia; Aunt Kate and Mary Jane – are visible here for a time.

The section builds to a climax with Gabriel's after-dinner speech: a complex mixture of the formal, ritualistic world of oratory and the private, personal world of family life. Gabriel's nervousness and his fears of personal failure have been described throughout but his speech (with, or perhaps despite, its careful refusal of 'gloomy moralising', its elegant and extended classical allusion and its sense of measured timing) is received well enough. It is after all a situation in which even Freddy Malins (or perhaps Freddy Malins especially) could have succeeded. Robert Browning, whose poetry famously features speakers whose monologues serve to reveal vital flaws in their characters, is the literary context offered to us by Gabriel's much-pondered quotation about the 'thought-tormented age'. No doubt it backfires on him. Although the phrase may be couched as a rebuke to Molly Ivors, it is Gabriel who is the most profoundly 'thought-tormented' of Joyce's Dubliners and who is, in this respect, the most revealing symptom of the age.

LOVE LETTERS

The third section of the story begins with the end of the party. Joyce describes the departures of the guests, then follows Gabriel and Gretta to the Gresham Hotel where they are to stay the night. Released from the dinner table, Gabriel is at last relaxed and spontaneously tells a story about his grandfather, a story that does not seem to have very much of a point (unless it is a point about absurdity and pointlessness) but still makes everybody laugh.

Lingering echoes of the evening are still in the air and Gretta is pictured leaning on those still-significant banisters, listening to the 'distant music' of Bartell D'Arcy and Miss O'Callaghan at the piano. Joyce's synaesthesia (describing the look of this audible scene) packs a powerful sensual and emotional punch. This is reinforced by the repetition of the phrase and deepened and made profoundly ambiguous by the narrative self-reference conveyed in Gabriel's thought: '*Distant Music* he would call the picture if he were a painter', and the disturbing literary self-consciousness of the fact that he himself wonders what she may be 'a symbol of'.

The subtlest inflections of the narrative carry enormous potential significance. When Gabriel first sees Gretta she is not named and so seems strange and unfamiliar: 'A woman was standing near, and he notes the 'grace and mystery' of her attitude. Her strangeness and the sight of her walking with Bartell D'Arcy make him faintly suspicious but also fire a little of the passion that has been absent in him up to this point: a passion that is communicated in the imagery of a 'wave', a 'flood' and of the 'soul'.

Gabriel remembers love letters that he wrote to Gretta in their youth and quotes a rhetorical question from one of them: '*Why is it that words like these seem to me to be so dull and cold. Is it because there is no word tender enough to be your name?*' Within the fictional illusion Gabriel's nostalgic echoes resonate, but Joyce is a modern writer in a time when a writer's privacy was fast becoming public property. The love letters he himself wrote to Nora at the start of their relationship have survived and have been published, and we can trace these very phrases back to two letters of 16 and 26 September 1904 (*SL*, 29, 31), which throw Gabriel's feelings into a different light.

Joyce's letters to Nora were not meant to be literature in the sense of Gabriel's after-dinner quotations from Browning or his *Daily Express* reviews, nor are they literary in the way that Casaubon's love letter to Dorothea in *Middlemarch* may be said to have literary affectation. They were not written for publication but to pursue private, physical and emotional goals in a personal relationship. Yet, like those of Browning, they are inescapably part of his writings and they show Joyce dealing with certain important literary ideas: trying to puzzle out the relationship between language and the body; locked in a fascinating struggle to articulate physical love when physical love by its very nature transforms language into non-linguistic bodily contact. 'I know', he wrote, 'that when I meet you next our lips will become mute' (*SL*, 31).

The question that both Joyce and Gabriel ask in their love letters is a rhetorical question, serving to reassure the woman addressed that she is, indeed, loved. But, like all rhetorical questions, it may provoke just the answer it seeks to pre-empt. Both possible answers to the question need to be considered, and need surely to be considered in relation to the second group of letters Joyce wrote to Nora in 1909, especially since one of the first of those letters (28 August 1909, *SL*, 163) referred Nora back to 'The Dead' and others to her Galway lover (*SL*, 183, 188), suggesting that Joyce thought of the letters as closely related to the story.

The first answer to the question might provide reassurance that a pure, disinterested 'tenderness' can be extraordinarily difficult to articulate in words, and perhaps Joyce came close to it in repeating in these later letters a description of Nora as 'My beautiful wild flower of the hedges! My dark-blue, rain-drenched flower!' and by his repeated reference to the famous passionate soprano aria from Puccini's *Madame Butterfly* 'Un Bel Di' (*SL*, 180–1, 188, 193 and 173–4, 195).

But another answer is also possible. This answer might note a touch of contradiction in the 'tender fires' that burn in Gabriel's thoughts or might see 'tenderness' itself as only a part of the passionate physical love that words may always strive and always fail to express. Conventional tenderness was only one part of the violently contradictory and exuberantly perverse desires that flooded from Joyce's passionate soul in these letters he wrote when he was separated from Nora in 1909. Alongside his 'spiritual love' he admits to a 'wild beast-like craving for every inch of your body, for every secret and shameful part of it, for every odour and act of it' (*SL*, 181). Must not the ever-present reality of this other kind of love also be a reason why Gabriel's decent and decorous words seem even to him to be 'dull and cold'?

In the letter of 22 August 1909 (*SL*, 163) Joyce gives a phrase from 'The Dead' an unmistakeably autobiographical gloss, referring to the three adjectives 'musical and strange and perfumed' as being used 'in speaking about your [i.e. Nora's] body'. It is those three qualities of the touch of Gretta's body that inspire in Gabriel 'a keen pang of lust' – a lust so strong he has to press his fingernails into his palms as they walk upstairs. Desires to 'crush her body against his' and to 'overmaster' rage in his mind and they are only quelled when they encounter the stronger passion in Gretta's confession of her experience of the passion of Michael Furey who she believes died for love of her.

Such passions are not articulated in the same way in the story as in Joyce's private letters which afford us a rare glimpse into the kind of 'secret life' that is only alluded to in the story. But there are allusions and they suggest the context in which Gabriel's psychology of failure and withdrawal should be read. 'Is the fire hot, sir?' he calls out to the man at the furnace in another rhetorical question whose erotic and infernal overtones hardly need to spelled out.

Joyce's language probes into areas that Sigmund Freud defined as the territory of dreams, jokes, fears and mistakes, and it can play strange tricks with a reader's mind. Perhaps we may learn something even from accidents of textual corruption that have characterised the history of Joyce's writing. Gabriel and Gretta settle in their hotel bedroom and he watches her get undressed in (what we can now read as another surfacing of the subtle Gothic thread) a 'ghostly light'. But the phrase was misread and reprinted in all editions up to 1967 as a 'ghastly light'. How suggestive a misreading this is, since the threatening eruption of a 'lust' that is angry, violent, perverse and possessive and may be even more threatening and dangerous in Gabriel's suppression of it, introduces such a 'ghastly' subtext to the story.

The question of secrecy can hardly be ignored. Joyce's letters bring into public gaze what is described in this story and certainly was for nineteenth-century Britain a 'secret life' of sexual activities and sexual desires. But that secret is no secret anymore and speaks of the great and paradoxical revolution of the twentieth century whereby, to look at the English press, for instance, a 'public' (that is, political) matter may well be confined to the 'serious papers' where it is read by a select audience of secretly powerful or at least responsible citizens, whereas a 'secret' is something that is avidly read by millions in the tabloids and has pictures and banner headlines to boot. An inner logic in the movement of democratic education and mass-reading seems to underlie this curious and worryingly de-democratising situation. The powerless mass are believed to have no substantial 'public' life or sustained interest in it. Their life is believed to be all 'private', all a 'secret', and their reading matter is 'private' to match. Concurrently the 'public' figure is supposed to lack a 'secret' or private life and when discovered to have one after all can (as we have seen in the replay of Victorian scandals that appeared in English political life in the 1980s) be forced to leave public office.

Joyce's love letters and his writing of 'The Dead' stand on two sides of that fence but peep through and typically anticipate a time when the fence may work the other way around. Joyce could have ended his story on an 'epiphany' with the guilty recognition that Gabriel feels on hearing of Michael Furey's passion and his sudden fears about the feebleness of 'his own clownish lusts', but he did not. Gabriel's rebuff from Gretta is the third 'discomposure' he suffers at the hands of a woman in the story and as with the other two Gabriel is shown in a third flight or escape: a flight worthy of the legendary Irish King Sweeney into the imaginative, poetic world of the coda.

This final passage seems inexhaustibly rich and rewarding to read and to analyse: as a piece of male sexual psychology, as spiritual or philosophical experience, as literary language, as fictional form and so on. The passage still has extraordinary power to move and to disturb. A traditional analysis might note Gabriel's repeated affirmations that build to a restrained climax, the trick of personification that makes the snow tap on the window like ghostly fingers, or the partial chiasmus that adds a warm but subtle note of closure to the final sentence. The animate and the inanimate merge throughout as Gabriel's identity fades into the 'grey impalpable' and deaths of the past and future pass before his eyes. The passage explores the human activity of imagination and has been read as a powerful vindication of the moral value of imagining by those who see in Gabriel the achievement of moral growth.

Positive moral terms do indeed figure here: Gabriel looks 'unresentfully' at Gretta and 'generous' tears fill his eyes. Yet it may be the Larkinian negative form in which they appear that governs the feeling of the passage and the manner in which Gabriel's affirmations are passed through a Freudian filter of denial: 'It hardly pained him now to think how poor a part . . .'.

The situation is an important one to which Joyce returned again and again in his writing: the situation of a husband's loving doubt about his wife. Much is explained by the fact that Gabriel's own consciousness is the medium through which the narrative communicates to us, contrasting with the broader or more multiple perspectives available earlier in the story. According to the decorum of this kind of narration, nothing he cannot see or imagine or know may be related to us and yet his testimony is far from reliable in this moment of extreme feeling as he 'swoons' and his very identity 'fades'. He only knows about Michael Furey at second hand, through Gretta's brief, uncertain and reluctantly offered memory of her girlhood romance. She herself may have romanticised or forgotten or may be editing to protect or even provoke her husband's feelings. He feels she knows something he does not but she is 'fast asleep' and cannot be called upon to supply corroboration or denial.

Neither Gabriel nor the reader of the story will ever know the final truth. There is a gap, a bottomless residue of doubt in the record, which Gabriel communicates through a rhetorical figure of assumed uncertainty: 'Perhaps she had not told him all the story.' Interestingly the gap in Gabriel's understanding is promptly filled with objects: 'A petticoat string dangled to the floor. One boot stood upright, its limp upper fallen down: the fellow of it lay upon its side.' What could speak more clearly of the other crucial absence at this point in the story: the sexual consummation that has not taken place between Gabriel and his wife. 'Better pass boldly into that other world in the full glory of some passion' thinks Gabriel, though he does not put this thought into action himself.

At the climax of his reverie 'generous tears' fill Gabriel's eyes and he seems to gain an intuition about love and a sense that he has never really been in love himself. He has decentred himself from his wife's experience and in a certain way from his own experience too. He gains a surprising vision, but has this extraordinary moment of 'grey, impalpable' self-dissolution and the Dantean glimpse of Furey's dripping wet ghost really got much to do with what Furey himself must have felt for Gretta?

One thing that seems crucial is the title. What might Joyce have meant by calling his story 'The Dead'? On the simplest, most literal level, it is the story of Gretta's dead lover: a ghostly revenant who haunts the story no less than the image of the dead priest in 'The Sisters'. But we should not forget the other ghost, the ghost of the significantly absent third Morkan sister, Gabriel's stern mother, who struggled for family respectability, who saddled him with his angelic name, who offered 'sullen opposition to his marriage', who has been photographed in the act of condemning her other son into the priesthood and who has also died.

There are the deathly monks of Mount Melleray who sleep in their coffins to remind them and the reader of the 'last end'. The 'late lamented' Patrick Morkan, Gabriel's grandfather and his horse Johnny are both brought back to life in Gabriel's story, and there is Aunt Julia who will be a ghost in the none too distant future.

But the title seems to imply a still more general or symbolic field of reference. Nothing is more important than the dead in Irish society. Even in the field of political action the Irish dead have often dominated the living – as the roll-call of the Nationalist dead in Yeats's *Kathleen ni Houlihan* or the case of Parnell in 'Ivy Day in the Committee Room' make clear. To reach near to the dead may be to achieve a high form of spiritual life (though it may also be to clog the living world with guilt and anxiety and despair). Gabriel's world of literature is another world subject to the possible liberating wisdom and the possible tyrannies of 'the dead'.

Here the wisdom and tyranny of the dead enter the politics of personal or private life. Michael Furey, whose autobiographical basis in a Michael Bodkin whom Nora Joyce once knew is clear from Joyce's letters, becomes a symbol of all lost or secret love (*SL*, 183 and 201). It is a ghost of love that the possessive instincts of the husband may seek to exorcise, but Joyce's most ambitious lovers, Richard Rowan in *Exiles* and Leopold Bloom in *Ulysses*, also seek to exorcise the ghost of possessiveness itself. Henchy's poem to the dead Parnell in 'Ivy Day' serves to stimulate new nationalistic longing. Joyce's erotic psychology is complex enough to show the memory of Michael Furey acting as a stimulus to Gabriel's lust. Furey himself may be literally dead, but in terms of erotic passion it is the other characters in the story who are dead and not him.

The extraordinarily multiform and uninhibited lust that Joyce expressed in his letters to Nora is absent from the magical and poetical ending of the story. Perhaps this is what makes those letters 'private' and Joyce's fiction 'literature'. Or perhaps in this as much as anything Gabriel's swooning soul has 'approached that region where dwell the vast hosts of the dead' and in this respect what Joyce meant by being 'dead' was exactly the opposite of what Lawrence meant by being 'alive'.

READING LIST

John D. and Ruth A. Boyd, 'The Love Triangle in James Joyce's "The Dead"', *University of Toronto Quarterly*, vol. 42, no. 3, (Spring 1973) pp. 202–17.

Anthony Burgess, 'City of Paralysis', *Here Comes Everybody* (London: Faber, 1965) pp.35–47.

Kenneth Burke, 'Three definitions', *Kenyon Review*, vol. 13, no. 2 (Spring 1951) pp. 173–92.

Clive Hart (ed.), *Dubliners: Critical Essays* (London: Faber, 1969).

Hugh Kenner, *Joyce's Voices* (London: Faber, 1978).

Marvin Magalaner, *Time of Apprenticeship* (New York: Abelard–Schuman, 1959).

W. J. McCormack, *Ascendancy and Tradition in Anglo-Irish Literature* (Oxford: Oxford University Press, 1984).

Jean-Michel Rabaté, 'Silence in *Dubliners*', in *James Joyce: New Perspectives*, ed. Colin MacCabe (Brighton: Harvester, 1982) pp. 45–72.

Frances Restuccia, *James Joyce and the Law of the Father* (Newhaven, Conn.: Yale, 1990).

Donald Torchiana, *Backgrounds for Joyce's 'Dubliners'* (Boston: Allen and Unwin, 1986).

Florence Walzl and Burton A. Waisbren, 'Paresis and the Priest: James Joyce's symbolic use of syphilis in "The Sisters"', *Annals of Internal Medecine*, vol. 80, no. 6 (June 1974) pp. 758–62.

Craig Werner, *Dubliners: A Pluralistic World* (New York: Twayne, 1988).

2
A Portrait of the Artist as a Young Man

A PORTRAIT OF THE READER AS CRITICAL THEORIST

There is little or nothing in Joyce's letters that justifies or explains *A Portrait of the Artist*. At the time of its first appearance as a serial in *The Egoist* Joyce was still busily engaged in the justification of *Dubliners* and perhaps the best record of the critical views that informed its composition is to be found in the body of writings and lectures made by Joyce during his residence in Trieste. These writings (sadly now out of print in England) include the lecture 'Ireland, Island of Saints and Sages', which gives the clearest account of Joyce's views of contemporary Ireland as a country defeated in spirit by centuries of English domination and by Roman Catholicism. Readers may better understand Stephen's discussions with Davin in *A Portrait* in the light of its vision of Ireland during the Parnell Home Rule era as a country capable only of moral narrowness and betrayal, and Joyce's view that 'no one who has any self-respect stays in Ireland' seems identical to Stephen's.

Joyce's choices of Defoe and Blake as examples from the English tradition informed the stark realism of the domestic sections of the novel and the embattled libertarian stance of its hero respectively. Joyce chose to lecture in 1907 (as he had done in 1902) on the nineteenth-century Irish poet James Clarence Mangan 'whose vices were exotic and whose patriotism was not very ardent'. The depth of Joyce's sympathy for Mangan's Romanticism goes some way toward explaining the indulgent lyricism of Stephen's poetry and his imaginings in *A Portrait*.

Typically, in politics and literature, Joyce defends the Irishman who has been the victim of narrow condemnation for immorality. So frequently does this position recur that one might suppose that Joyce felt that moral transgression might be intrinsic to the artistic process. Such is the position outlined in the most important of the pieces for the understanding of *A Portrait*: the essay on Oscar Wilde that he wrote on the occasion of a performance of Strauss's operatic version of Wilde's *Salomé* in 1909 in Trieste. Here Joyce indicates his dislike of the public school system, which he portrays as harsh and unsympathetic in *A Portrait*, and in his own heavily theological terms he spells out the artistic need to trangress and rebel:

Here we touch the pulse of Wilde's art – sin (*CW*, 204). Joyce's tone throughout the essay is sympathetic to Wilde but his words might almost be read as an account of the trials and ambitions of his own artist figure Stephen:

> He deceived himself into believing that he was the bearer of good news of neo-paganism to an enslaved people. His own distinctive qualities, the qualities perhaps of his race – keenness, generosity, and a sexless intellect – he placed at the service of a theory of beauty which, according to him, was to bring back the Golden Age and the joy of the world's youth. But if some truth adheres to his subjective interpretations of Aristotle, to his restless thought that proceeds by sophisms rather than syllogisms, to his assimilations of natures as foreign to his as the delinquent is to the humble, at its very base is the truth inherent in the soul of Catholicism: that man cannot reach the divine heart except through that sense of separation and loss which is called sin.   (*CW*, 204–5)

Joyce's critical writing often adopts a semi-biographical approach to its subject and we might start by recognising that his *Portrait of the Artist* is made up of traces of these other portraits of artists' lives. Stephen, no less than Wilde, has to sin. But it is more usually as a portrait of himself that Joyce's novel has been treated. This has generated much interesting discusssion about the literary genre of autobiography and *A Portrait* has been shown to be both auto-biographical fiction in the very literal sense that Joyce used the material of his own life as subject (Parrinder, 1984) and to be a fiction about the literary artist and therefore a fiction that is in some sense about itself (Butler, 1984; Riquelme, 1989).

Some of this discussion has traced the idea of writing an autobiographical fiction to the curious draft essay that Joyce had unsuccesfully submitted to the periodical *Dana* before he left Dublin in 1904 and to some letters from 1904–5 that refer to the novel of which a fragment survives as *Stephen Hero* (Scott, 1986; Parrinder, 1984). Joyce's revision of that wordy draft into the orderly brilliance of the novel has seemed a paradigm both of the imaginative distance required of a mature literary artist and of the radical contemporary transition from Edwardian to Modernistic aesthetics (Booth, 1983).

The existence of these early drafts should remind us that here as ever Joyce was engaged on a work in progress and that from his early poetry *Chamber Music* and *Dubliners* through his play *Exiles* and posthumously published prose-poem *Giacomo Joyce* and on to *Finnegans Wake*, Joyce was engaged in a continual rewriting and reprojection of himself. In this his autobiography (as Roy Pascal pointed out long ago) has nothing to do with those retrospective memoirs of great public men that are sometimes also called autobiographies. His genre is the fictional genre of self-translation and self-discovery.

As a modern autobiography, critics have compared *A Portrait* to the portraits of young men and writers in George Gissing, Samuel Butler and Edmund Gosse, to Lawrence's *Sons and Lovers*, to Woolf's *Jacob's Room* (Lawrence, 1986), to the displaced figure of the author in Mann's *Death in Venice* (Butler, 1984), to the celebratory aesthetic vision of Gide's *Immoralist*, the self-conscious autobiographical layering of *The Counterfeiters* and the ironised egoists in the fiction of George Meredith. Terms like *Bildungsroman* (the German term for a novel of education and upbringing) and *Künstlerroman* (a term coined to label novels with artists as heroes) have been used to define it, but too much emphasis on the old Victorian concept of the artist as a hero can be a mistake since *A Portrait* is also the first modern novel and in this it might be said that its real hero is not so much the élite cult figure of the artist as the universally relevant figure of the critically active reader. It may be the discovery or construction of the heroic critical reader, as much as of that of the heroic creative artist, that it subtly explores.

It has often been noted that Stephen's one artistic production, the empty and repetitive *villanelle* he produces in Chapter Five, is not much on which to base his claim to be a great poet. In order to justify him as an 'artist' the reader has to imagine him as the future author of Joyce's novel. We might surely take a lead here from Oscar Wilde's famous essay on 'The Critic as Artist' that was certainly well known to Joyce. Stephen's mind, as its further development shown in *Ulysses* confirms, is a creative organ from which he is able to produce brilliant fragments and flashes of literary theory and he is constantly embroiled in literary theoretical debate. The literary-critical essay that wins a school prize in Chapter Two is the only piece of his creative writing that becomes public in the sense that it earns him any money. Stephen is a reader as much as a writer, a kind of 'semblable' or 'frère' to the reader addressed by Baudelaire (Rabaté, 1991). Joyce's novel may provide a central character who is not so much an aloof or disdainful 'priestlike' artist, as a vehicle for the demystification of such authority, both a symbolic model and an empowering vindication of the role of the reader, encouraging him or her into full self-expressive life.

Some recent developments in criticism may be understood as a gradual recognition of the importance of this shift of emphasis toward the reader. While in the 1950s and 1960s the novel's ideal coherence and consistency might have been praised, we can now see more clearly the importance of its episodic and fragmentary qualities, its imbrication of many styles and languages which inspire an active readerly construction of meaning and order. Providing neither a fixed narratorial perspective nor a moral point of view, and having no clearly imposed ending to close off the potential directions of its narrative, *A Portrait* has above all invited debate.

The fact that one of the most pervasive and longest lasting of these debates concerns Stephen himself – the extent to which we are to understand him as authorial surrogate; the extent to which we can take him at his own estimate of himself; whether he is to be understood as a Daedalus or only an Icarus – should not deflect us from the realisation that he may also serve as a surrogate of the reader's intellectual activities, especially those activities that have made the educated reader him or herself into one of the intellectual heroes of the post-modern age.

Joyce further weds Stephen's experience to that of the reader by his insistence on portraying Stephen's intellectual development alongside the development of his heterosexuality. Some feminist critics have attacked both Joyce and Stephen in these terms, arguing that Joyce 'supports patriarchy' (Lawrence, 1986), that the Emma Clery described in *Stephen Hero* is a much more fully realised female role than the shadowy universalised girls of Stephen's dreams in *A Portrait* (Scott, 1986) or else that the novel is merely a portrait of a young misogynist (Henke, 1990). Others, though, have begun to explore deeper psychological significances of the relationship between language and sexuality in the portrayal of Stephen's mind: significances that may be relevant for men and women too (Ellmann, 1982).

This area is not, after all, a subtheme but an essential part of a book which tries to explore and define the nature of the aesthetic life. Stephen's own theories of the 'esthetic' may not fully conceptualise it, but this very mixture of the artistic and sexual takes us right back to the origins of the term 'aesthetic' which designated all that territory of human experience governed by the senses as opposed to the intellect: that part of experience that is so oddly left out in the familiar Cartesian formula for existence: 'I think therefore I am.'

The concentration on sexuality in *A Portrait* sits at an important moment in the history of society and ideas, whether we interpret that history as a change from Victorian sexual 'repression' to modern sexual 'liberation' or whether we accept the position adopted by Michel Foucault that there has been a massive increase in discursive activity in this area which may imply a potentially repressive continuum between the sex-control of institutions like the Catholic Church confessional, the growth of a morally repressive nineteenth-century sexual science and all our obsessive modern talk about sex. Joyce's Catholic upbringing gave him an insight into one aspect of this; his Swiftian attention to obscenity and outrage and his Blakean desires for liberation mixed into a modern consciousness that kept him abreast of the discoveries of the Freudian unconscious and of contemporary sexual science. *A Portrait* remains a key text in this history, not least because of the way that it portrays sex as an integral part of language and art in the area of aesthesis that it strives to define.

A Portrait can also be seen as an important site of other kinds of social change. H. G. Wells in an early review was one of the first to comment on its importance for a world where the novel was beginning to take more and more of life into its territorial control. *A Portrait* that exploration and transgression of the boundaries between the public and the private life, between the outside and the inside of a character's experience that was already and was to become still further the accepted hallmark of Joyce's art.

These important areas of social change, characteristic of our time, may have been insufficiently explored in relation to *A Portrait* by social and culturalist critics who have been divided in their sense of its importance thus far. While some (like early Eagleton) drew an identity between artistic exile, the trials of the alienated citizen and/or the perspective of the radical critic of society, others (like Raymond Williams and Arnold Kettle) tended to avoid a novel that seems so exclusively focused on a single bourgeois sensibility and might therefore fall foul of Lukácsian and other critiques of the modernist novel. Still others seek out the traces of Joyce's own sympathies for early twentieth-century socialist, anarchist and nationalist thought in *Stephen Hero* and in his Italian writings, regretting their apparent excision from *A Portrait* (Manganiello, 1980). But Joyce's self-education in socialistic thought pays off in *A Portrait* all the same. Undeniably Stephen is an isolated figure but his isolation is always seen in the social contexts that produce it: the contexts of school, the priestly life, the domestic life, the father–son relationship, the university and so on. We are given sympathetic insight into his feelings and perceptions, but his ideas are always presented socially – as part of a debate. The nationalist and socialist perspectives of Stephen's contemporaries are given a clear voice in the text if not the vote of Stephen himself.

There is an undeniable economic determinism in the presentation of action and structure in *A Portrait,* moving from the wealth of the young family whose first-born son goes to one of the most expensive public boarding schools in Ireland to the domestic squalor of the university years. Indeed his growing literary ambitions in relation to a declining economic state might well serve as a hidden analogy to the paradigm familiar in the 'great house' novels of the Anglo-Irish literary tradition of a high ideal of literature that is in some ways both product and echo of the declining economic power of a nation or a social class.

Contemporary Marxist revisionism, with its stress on the materiality of language and psychology and on the primacy of the ideological over the material struggle (MacCabe, 1978) has had a great deal more to say on *A Portrait* but the full recognition within all of these debates of Stephen's role as a figural model for the reader as modern intellectual hero and of *A Portrait* as the primary location for a post-Cartesian redefinition of the aesthetic is only beginning to emerge.

ONCE UPON A TIME

The centrality of aesthesis to *A Portrait* is evident from the snatch of nursery language and association that makes up the sensational opening of its very first page. The language seems to hover on the threshold of the non- or pre-linguistic: 'When you wet the bed, first it is warm then it gets cold. His mother put on the oilsheet. That had the queer smell. His mother had a nicer smell than his father' (*P*, 7).

The analogy between Stephen and the experience of the reader is also established. The reader is confronted with the complex and ambiguous verbal signs of a Latin epigraph, a word-salad of unexplained personal associations and obscure snatches of rhyme. Stephen, likewise, is introduced as a listener to his father's puzzling narrative, attempting to work out his own place in it:

> Once upon a time and a very good time it was there was a moocow coming down along the road and this moocow that was coming down along the road met a nicens little boy named baby tuckoo . . . .
> His father told him that story: his father looked at him through a glass: he had a hairy face.
> He was baby tuckoo. (*P*, 7)

According to some critics this snatch of narrative represents a patriarchal order of authority that the young boy must learn to overthrow in order to establish his own 'story', his own version of the truth (Riquelme, 1989). It does at any rate locate him from the start as a reader in a world that is already full of texts, who seeks for but does not yet possess a full meaning of the signs around him. Both he and the reader are set adrift into a Daedalian labyrinth of sense impressions, half remembered riddling nursery rhymes, conundrums of familial, religious and political origin and loyalty, contradictory desires and constraints.

Each item opens up a trail of possible enquiry: contextual, intertextual, biographical, political, psychological, theological, and so on. The reader must at once be open to and on guard against the chains of association that seem to promise some final explanation of all these terms, since to gain any such explanation would be to lose the sense of disorder and mystery that is central to the experience described. It is all too easy to replace real discontinuities with supposed coherences. Equally we must resist the temptations to think of it purely as a kind of musical overture or exercise in 'style'.

Organised into chapters and episodes (along the lines of a five-act play) the disciplined structure of *A Portrait* occupies the foreground. No sooner has the nursery world been established than we break with crisp montage to a second scene: a 'day-in-the-life' of Stephen as a nine year old – close in age and temperament to the boy of the first *Dubliners* stories – at boarding school.

A vestigial narrative voice apparently gives us a descriptive fix on the circumstantial experience of this school: the playgrounds 'swarming' with boys; the hour for sums; the refectory; the playroom; the studyhall; the chapel; the dormitory and the infirmary. But the voice we remember most of all is the voice of the boy himself as he experiences these things in actuality or – increasingly throughout the novel – as he constructs and controls narrative selection and pro-gression in anticipation or retrospection through a filter of memory, fantasy and desire. His innocence is our guide as he tries to come to terms with the world according to the 'authority' of what he has been told ('That was not a nice expression. His mother had told him not to speak with the rough boys at college. Nice mother!' *P*, 9) or according to the associations of his own curiosity (the coincidence of colour between Dante's two brushes and the earth and clouds of Fleming's picture). But, especially on re-reading, the boy's own innocence posits an implied author and implied readers with a correspondingly well-developed sophistication.

His sexual innocence ('Was it right to kiss his mother or wrong to kiss his mother?' *P*, 15) implies a classic Oedipal conundrum. His struggle with naming ('God was God's name just as his name was Stephen' *P*, 16) inaugurates a debate about language and identity that grows into a major theme of the book. His ignorance of politics ('It pained him that he did not know well what politics meant' *P*, 17) conceals a highly sophisticated tracery of political implications embedded in the labyrinth of his thoughts. First among these is his shadowy, sickbed intimation of the death of Parnell, whose political failure was the most significant event in recent Irish history.

The narrative jumps from school to home but instead of Stephen returning to the warm maternal images of 'nice mother' and 'feet on the fender', he is thrust into a political debate over Christmas dinner that goes beyond the vividness of the dinner in 'The Dead' and the garrulous political drama of 'Ivy Day in the Committee Room'. In the 1890s the alliance of Parnell and Gladstonian liberalism briefly held out the prospect of a united Ireland given meaningful Home Rule without recourse to violent uprising. It may not be an over-simplification to say that the collapse of this consensus, resulting from an outrage over Parnell's adultery on a scale that it is difficult for a modern reader to comprehend, led ultimately to the religious sec-tarianism, insurrectionary bloodletting and partition of Ireland that still defy resolution today.

Without a trace of the adult attitudinising that would cloud the objective reporting of the child's innocent eye, we are given a clear map of this consensual fracture at work. Beneath the genteel surface war has broken out. Simon Dedalus entertains a Mr Casey who has just been in prison 'making a birthday present for Queen Victoria', apparently in connection with his fiercely held Home Rule loyalties that soon become the subject of violent dinner table debate. He defends Parnell, while Dante Riordan, the family nurse, puts across the morally censorious Irish Catholic Church view that brought Parnell down. Her name (on an innocent level a childish corruption of 'Auntie') reminds us of the other Dante who attempted a large-scale defence of the world view of the Catholic Church. She, though, is a Dante reduced to a prudish late nineteenth-century idea of 'respectable' sexual propriety: a Dante whose creation of heaven and hell offered a carrot and stick for contemporary moralisers that might be thought of as another 'birthday present for Queen Victoria'.

Casey is by no means constrained by gentlemanly ideals. He has spat in the eye of an 'old harridan' who has heckled him and called Kitty O'Shea a whore, and he tells the story deliberately to provoke Dante, startling the young boy into a typical reaction that it was 'not nice'. Mr Dedalus (Stephen's parents are called by their surnames throughout, which seems to distance this scene from the child's perception of it) is clearly sympathetic to Casey and his position. Mrs Dedalus (the mother whose love so dominates Stephen's image of the home) is at first silent in the scene, but she does speak up against political disagreement and ultimately betrays herself as rather sympathetic to Dante's defence of the priestly morality of chastity and repression.

The political war is thus crossed through with a sex war glimpsed by Scott, Parrinder and others. The men are untroubled by the sexual freedom of Parnell and Kitty O'Shea in relation to the prospect of political progress, but a violent matriarchy (or internalised 'patriarchy'?) holds sway which cannot accept any infringement of the domestic law of 'God and morality and religion come first!' and which revels in vengeful condemnation: 'Devil out of hell! We won! We crushed him to death! Fiend!'

The defeat of Parnell by Irish moral matriarchy may have other implications for the young Stephen. Some historians, taking a clue from W. B. Yeats's lyric 'Come Gather Round Me Parnellites', have argued that the political consensus represented by Parnell did not disappear entirely but was transformed into the kind of consensus implied by the flourishing of an Anglo-Irish literature and literary audience at the start of the century, of which the arrival of Yeats's new National Theatre at the centre of European cultural life and the literary/sexual aesthesis of Joyce were both parts.

In the final section of the first chapter a number of ingredients are added to the mix, developing the treatment of Stephen's sexual feelings and allowing him brief prominence as what is, perhaps, a new kind of political hero whose very feelings are set up against the hierarchical 'justice' meted out by the teacher/priests of the school.

Stephen overhears the other boys talking in a secret jargon about some schoolboy crime. The boys have 'scut', but why? Is it because they have 'fecked' the communion wine or because they have been caught 'smugging' in the square? (*P*, 43). Is 'smugging' some kind of stealing, perhaps plagiarism (as the *OED* interestingly indicates) or, as some readers have thought, a schoolboy sexual peccadillo of some masturbatory or homosexual kind? Sexual crime or literary crime, 'smugging' provides another linguistic mystery for Stephen's curious imaginings and those of the reader to pursue.

Stephen's train of thought turns to other mysteries of the 'sacristy', its 'crimped surplices' and dressing up as 'boatbearer', connecting them with the half-understood exploratory sexual touching of the Eileen Vance of the opening and with thoughts of her sexuality linked to images of the Virgin Mary. Mysteriously these feelings are linked to the feeling of punishment – not in an easy moral framework but as part of a more complex psychic economy of pleasure and pain: 'There were different kinds of pains for all the different kinds of sounds', he thinks.

Joyce may be providing an anatomy of the ways in which the 'secrecy and restrictions' of a certain kind of school system (as he hints in his Oscar Wilde essay) might be said to produce such sexual orientations as masochism and homosexuality, and of the ways in which religious imageries participate in the construction of his heterosexuality.

This whole complex of feelings is interrupted by the bullying prefect Father Dolan, who breaks into the class looking for boys to beat with the fearsome 'pandybat' and picks on Stephen. At the egging of his fellows and feeling as if he is truly one with them at last, Stephen complains to the rector and by persistent questioning and explanation achieves a victory over the school's regime of punishment and authority.

We still feel the naïvety of Stephen's thought through a subtle control of syntax and prose rhythm: 'The prefect of studies was a priest but that was cruel and unfair', but the logic and structure of feeling in the episode requires that we accept the justice of Stephen's feelings over the tyrannical hegemony of the teachers and priests who make up so much of his experience of the adult world.

The politics of Stephen's position as a parodic Tribune in this miniature revolution is not clear. In an early essay he wrote 'No man can be a lover of the true and the beautiful who does not abhor the multitude' and we cannot help noticing that there is more than a hint of snobbery or priggishness in his triumph: 'Dolan: it was like the name of a woman that washed clothes.' More than simple democracy the victory of new kinds and structures of feeling seems to be offered to us here.

These are the incidents dramatised in this first chapter, but one corollary of the strategy of filtering the narrative through Stephen's private life, personality and memory is that most of the conventionally important key events happen off-stage, as it were, in the gaps. Between the opening and the second scene Stephen has grown and been sent to school, but on the eve of the football match scene, he has been pushed into the 'square ditch' by the bully Wells. Between his illness of that evening and the Christmas dinner scene the death of Parnell has become the dominant element in pre-revolutionary Irish political debate. Between the Christmas vacation of 1891 and the final scene in Chapter One the boys have been caught 'smugging' and Stephen has broken his glasses, both incidents preparing for his adopted posture against tyranny, injustice and pain at the end of the chapter.

The very absence of these events gives them a centrality to what follows that is unmatched by any 'present' event. The language of *A Portrait* no less than that of *Dubliners* hinges on gaps and silences and absences that may be unknown or else, even if known, be crucially undecidable.

VICE VERSA

Whatever hopes Stephen may have of achieving some kind of order are dashed by the shifting of the ground on which he stands. Between chapters Stephen's father's prosperity has declined. The servant-filled house of the Christmas dinner has become lodgings in Blackrock and Dublin with his Great-Uncle Charles where the furniture disappears; sumptuous Clongowes has turned into the workaday Christian Brothers School and only at the cost of some humiliation for Stephen does his father squeeze him into the tightly disciplined Jesuit day-school Belvedere. Social class is a slippery slope for the growing boy whose own adolescence now begins to press upon him. Social and sexual forces interact in the construction of his masculinity, which may be foregrounded as the theme of a chapter in which Stephen explores and outgrows the flawed models of paternity in his natural family and seeks out feminine alternatives that may allow him to transcend their limitations. 'He's not that way built' says Stephen's father, 'Leave him to his Maker' (*P*, 97): the temptations to analyse this construction of his sexuality are strong.

The two sections that recount his experiences in Blackrock and Dublin – the episode of the play in Stephen's new school and the trip with his father to Cork – are all coloured by issues of gender. First he tries out the men. Great-Uncle Charles is 'banished to the outhouse' for the very activity of smoking, which his nephew identifies as one of the daring and bonding masculine experiences in his own youth. Stephen 'lends an avid ear' to their talk. The old men try to train Stephen up as an athlete. With a male friend he forms a gang of adventurers and they play with the milkmen and the boys.

Then the trauma of the disappearing furniture turns him to his 'redeyed mother'. The male figures fall into decline and it is with her that he visits his Aunt Josephine and peers into a female world where 'the beautiful Mabel Hunter' reigns and in which he himself is mysteriously taken for Josephine. This subtly cross-gendered experience, allied to his new experience of the 'vastness and strangeness' of the city, coincides with – and is narrated by means of – Stephen's new writerly habit of detached observation in the prose sketch or 'epiphany' that was a cornerstone of the new aesthetic in *Stephen Hero*. We hear how he 'chronicled with patience what he saw, detaching himself from it and testing its mortifying flavour in secret' (*P*, 69).

Distance alone cannot produce any more than a priestly, emasculated and feebly compensatory art as the third incident (the encounter with the girl at the tram stop whom we never see except through her intials E—C—) clearly shows. Sensing a romantic opportunity, some aloofness and dubiety prevents him from acting on the impulse and he remains 'a tranquil watcher of the scene before him'. The next morning, in compensation, he writes a poem in which 'the kiss, which had been withheld by one, was given by both'. The inadequacy of the verse as an expression of Stephen's new aesthesis and the extent to which its chastity represents little more than the internalised authority he resists is suggested by the fact that 'from force of habit' he heads it with the Jesuit motto AMDG.

Such poetry is compensatory but not transgressive as Stephen learns two years later when the same girl appears at the school Whitsun play in the company of his father. Joyce himself performed in a farce by F. Anstey called *Vice Versa* in which a father and son change places for a time. In the fictionalised version Stephen's part of 'a farcical pedagogue' allows him to 'change places' with his teachers. Such transformations are tied up with an atmosphere of theatrical and priestly transvestism, stimulating an atmosphere of licence in which Stephen's desires are aroused and mocked by his schoolfellows who have spotted the girl in his father's company and who – as flashback piles on flashback – force him (only partly teasingly) to 'admit' that the 'greatest poet' Byron was, in the eyes of the priests, a great heretic too.

The presence of the girl maddens and inspires him, but the end of the episode leaves him devastated 'amid the suddenrisen vapours of wounded pride and fallen hope and baffled desire', attempting an almost ludicrous sensual self-mortification with the odour of 'horse piss and rotted straw'.

Stephen's visit to Cork with his father has been a favourite topic for recent critics who have found it a psychic crux for the construction of Stephen's writerly identity in relation to that of his father. The episode is a double quest. On the one hand the father seeks the assurance of his lost childhood, and on the other the son seeks for the mystery that will give him access to the desired authority of his father. The chapter hinges on his readerly search for the mysterious sign of Simon's initials carved on the desk of the anatomy theatre. For Riquelme the incident marks the place where Stephen's ability to narrate or imagine his own story first supplants the paternal narrative of the opening.

Maud Ellmann argues that the word *foetus* – which Stephen finds on the desk – traumatically reinforces the biological link of child to mother rather than the social or linguistic link of paternity that is implied by the identity of their two names, asserting matriarchal over patriarchal power.

Whether it represents the collapse of the whole patriarchal order (Scott, 1986; Ellmann, 1982) – or merely of particular bad examples of it (Tindall, 1959; Van Ghent, 1959) – the incident marks a transition in terms of money and sex. At first Simon revels in memories of his youth when he was 'the boldest flirt in the city of Cork', and that of his father who was 'the handsomest man in Cork at that time'. The last of his inherited wealth (the recovery of which is the main reason for his visit) inflates him. He is keen to show off and is fluent in a Cork idiom of 'lobs' and '*come-all-yous*' that is alien to a 'Dublin jackeen' like Stephen whose own inadequacies as a 'flirt' have just been shown up in a scene where even E—C— seems to have preferred his father's company to his own.

The sight of the word *foetus* primarily sparks off in Stephen a series of associations concerning the masturbatory 'reveries' and 'orgies' that, we now learn, are becoming a pressing feature of his life. The term is a rebuke since it reminds him both of his immaturity and also of the (matriarchally inspired?) guilts associated with the anti-utilitarian, non-reproductive anathema of the act at this time. The chain of associations reminds him of his weaknesses but also goads him into a recognition of his strengths: 'He recalled his own equivocal position in Belvedere, a free boy, a leader afraid of his own authority' (*P*, 94). Beside intimations of his intellectual success, his father's advice becomes reduced to that of a peer ('more like brothers than father and son'). It is predicted that Simon's vaunted physical prowess will be supplanted by Stephen's greater intellectual power. The old men enter a second childhood through drink while Stephen begins to age mysteriously until 'his mind seemed older than theirs'.

In the next episode Stephen's new generation has taken over from the old one in both money and love. By exercising his heretical talent for the writing of essays to the extent that he wins the substantial school essay prize, he has at least proposed that money and status can be earned by the exercise of the mind as well as inherited from the past: 'his trousers' pockets bulged with masses of gold and silver coins' (*P*, 100). In the second mock revolution of the book he sets himself up as the new head of the family, establishing a new economy along the lines of a 'commonwealth'. No longer a detached observer of his own longings he also establishes a new spiritual economy in which: 'Beside the savage desire within him to realise the enormities which he brooded on nothing was sacred' (*P*, 101).

This distinctive mixture of money, writing and sex leads Stephen on to the climax of the second chapter where he must confirm his reconstruction of himself in sexual as well as intellectual terms. More than the replacement of traditional images of male authority with new images of female desire is at stake in this stage of Stephen's development. There is also more than the instructive contrast between the vague, idealised female image of Mercedes with which Stephen has filled his imaginations in the early parts of the chapter, and the exploited prostitutes whom were all the priestbound morality and garrison status of the contemporary Dublin streets could provide by way of actuality.

The drama takes place at the level of aesthesis where the paralysis of detachment brought on by Stephen's intellectual self-discipline has given way to an irresolvable conflict between language and the body. We are told that 'his blood was in revolt' and in an image that must owe something to the late Victorian Gothic of a Stevenson, a Stoker or a Le Fanu he is possessed by 'some dark presence moving irresistibly upon him from the darkness, a presence subtle and murmurous as a flood filling him wholly with itself' (*P*, 102).

But Stephen is no Gothic sex fiend. Little in the powerfully distorting stereotypes of pornography or in the available morally charged late-Victorian discourses concerning prostitution and 'the rescue of fallen women' prepare us for the portrait of Stephen's sexual initiation or for the simple and straightforward young woman with whom he achieves it. Moral issues of prostitution are left to the reader to debate. In an attitude that he believed to be characteristic of that of Christ in the gospels, Joyce portrays the young woman with warmth and respect: the innocence suggested by the 'huge doll' in her room counterbalancing the 'proud conscious movements of her perfumed head' (*P*, 103).

A fever of language reflects the fever of Stephen's desire. Just as with Eileen Vance (who takes the active part in the sexual incident of his memory) and with E—C—, and indeed as Joyce himself (who gratefully remembers to Nora that 'it was you who slid your hand down down inside my trousers' *SL*, 182), Stephen does not take the active part. He may think he is a sex monster but actually he is a shy and sensitive boy whose body is denied in the complex intellectual languages he has learnt so well, and he is caught in an impossible dialectic of idealism and disgust. It is beyond language into the territory of the unspeakable or the ineffable defined by Joyce's letters to Nora that Stephen's ecstasy transgresses: 'his lips parted though they would not speak' (*P*, 103). In this territory beyond language he can transcend Cartesian duality and surrender 'body and mind' to the girl who provides an alternative language of the body in her lips that 'pressed upon his brain as upon his lips as though they were the vehicle of a vague speech' (*P*, 104), a speech that he cannot yet talk himself but is at least beginning to learn to read.

TO SAY IT IN WORDS

Stephen's attempt to learn the language of the female body ends in disillusion. He has discovered a new somatic territory but has no language to validate the experience beyond the 'drawling jargon' that marks its entrapment in the territory of the commercial and the illegitimate, and the moral framework of 'sin', which flavours the experience with shame and disgust. He has not yet found the means to transgress or disrupt the problematic separations that inhibit his conversations with E—C—. On the contrary his naïve idealisation of female inviolability seems to have increased. He has become a prefect of the school's cult of the Virgin Mary and he revels in the Pre-Raphaelite religiosity of Marian devotion. Joyce apparently learnt from the Catholic *Bildungsroman* of French woman writer Marcelle Tinayre (which he reviewed in 1903) of the pernicious 'double temperament' imposed in the contemporary constructions of masculinity, and he provides Stephen with a bad dose.

His new synthesis has become profoundly fractured. Access to economic, social and intellectual progress is through an educational advancement that focuses his attention on theological conundrum and increasingly demands a moral obedience. Unable to progress beyond the widening terms of this dialectic, he is ripe for the 'retreat' that

forms the terrifying middle section of this tripartite chapter and a
structural centre of the novel. 'A retreat', explains Father Arnall,
'signifies a withdrawal.' For Stephen it proves much more, representing a withdrawal from the female body into the emasculating
disciplines and orders of surrogate 'fathers' and it is a retreat from the
new aesthesis of his intellectual and sexual life. It is a regression into
the childhood world of Clongowes, from which Arnall has 'strangely
re-arisen' to deliver the sermons, and the idioms of his childish
thought recur.

The narrative idiom itself enacts an extraordinary withdrawal. The
familiar mixture of sympathetic narrative modulation and the free
associations of Stephen's thoughts are invaded by the parodied and
quoted collage of contemporary Jesuit thought, first echoing the
sensual Marian St Alphonsus Liguori, and then giving way almost
entirely to sermons based on the hell-raising Italian Jesuit Pinamonti.
In their wake Stephen's natural personal development is subsumed in
a self-torturingly meticulous new life of designer piety built from the
devotional exercises of St Ignatius Loyola. This is an especial
nightmare for Stephen as Loyola was the primary inspiration for the
evangelising of Francis Xavier, who was in turn the presiding genius
of the Jesuit order and hence of Stephen's college.

From a recent post-modern perspective it has been claimed that the
curiosity of this religious tradition may be more apparent to the reader
of *A Portrait* (even the modern Catholic reader) than the heroism of
Stephen's gestures of rejection and apostasy (Buttigeig, 1987). Joyce
puts this destructively organisational material in the foreground,
especially Arnall's horrific sermons, which for page after page
terrorise and gradually subvert Stephen's sensitive and susceptible
consciousness until his better judgement succumbs.

Words like 'sin' and 'indulgence', which were enriched with a
Baudelairean tinge for the emerging literary intellectual, are grabbed
back for pious orthodoxy with an almost mathematical zeal. Stephen's
'soul', which had come to suggest an expanding and exploratory seat
of his affections and desires is now only a cold receptacle for
prejudged good or evil deeds. Language is on the side of the
authorities that control it, implying a conspiratorial identity of word
and thing named, so that even the naughty boy whom Arnall rebukes
before his sermon is called 'Lawless'.

The theme of Arnall's sermon is the four last things: death, judgement, heaven and hell. It does not dwell specifically on sexual sin but Stephen's reactions to it are almost exclusively posed in terms of the sexual guilts that it generates:

> the sootcoated packet of pictures which he had hidden in the flue of the fireplace and in the presence of whose shameless or bashful wantonness he lay for hours sinning in thought and deed.   (*P*, 119)

On the eve of the first day's thoughts on 'death' and 'judgement', Stephen's 'cold lucid indifference' has turned to a 'thick fog'. By the end of the day the mere sound of a girl's laughter causes in him an 'agony of shame'. When it comes to hell, Arnall gets so deeply into his theme that Stephen's spirit has no courage or resistance left for the promised fourth and final part, which we never hear. This hell has none of the human tragedy of Dante's *Inferno*. It is a Sadeian fantasy of extreme psychic and physical pains. Indeed, according to Roland Barthes, de Sade, Fourier and Loyola are deeply coterminous in their thorough planning of schemes and systems to order the life of the body according to extreme forms of willed discipline and control.

This is precisely the regime that Stephen has internalised by the start of the fourth chapter. The potentially liberating ideas of past or future time – the flexible time in which Stephen's reveries could once freely play – have been attacked in the sermons by an absolutely constraining insistence on the present. 'Time is, time was, but time shall be no more' (*P*, 127). Stephen's actual time is now planned and divided into the structures and routines of his subjection. All sensual feeling is numbed in the alarming programme of self mortifications that he imposes on himself. That he plays a willing Masoch to Loyola's de Sade is probably suggested by the passage describing the 'feminisation' of his soul. 'This idea of surrender had a perilous attraction for his mind' and he begins to realise it as he gradually allows himself to become conscious of his stunted feelings once again (*P*, 155). Pain may replace pleasure as the object of unconscious desiring; it cannot eradicate desire.

In the scene leading up to his confession, where Stephen flees from the sermons to the privacy of his own room, we see the impact of this discursive hand-grenade on his sensitivity as a reader and interpreter of signs. Terrified, he hovers on the threshold of his dark room, a dark that he is now convinced must be the home of 'fiends'. He hears or mishears a chiasmatic babble of voices that can only indicate that a kind of paranoid state has been induced, which throws him into a mental reverse gear:

> We knew perfectly well of course that although it was bound to come to the light he would find considerable difficulty in endeavouring to try to induce himself to try to endeavour to ascertain the spiritual plenipotentiary and so we knew of course perfectly well.   (*P*, 139–40)

We may suppose what kinds of daemonic suggestion the words might have for Stephen as he tries to convince himself that they are merely nonsense and he calls up a vision, his own 'epiphany' of hell as a shit-spattered wasteland peopled by goat-like fiends whose 'soft language' and lips seem to have become associated with the 'vague speech' of the girl (*P*, 141). Mentally he castrates himself, imagining a remote centre of consciousness for that 'bestial part of his body', asking 'Was that then he or an inhuman thing?' and sickening at its 'torpid snaky life' (*P*, 143).

Loyolan 'consciousness of place' provides him now with no objective realistic space but only another 'Church Street'. All language conspires against him and Stephen can only stumble into this 'Church Street chapel' to confess. But in some sense the act of confession highlights the very problem that Stephen has been facing all along, for confession paradoxically requires that he put into language precisely what he did in order to escape from language, and that he find words to achieve a state of orthodoxy that is defined as having no words for these deeds: 'To say it in words! His soul, stifling and helpless, would cease to be' (*P*, 146).

If his first kiss and bodily climax seemed to Stephen to be a kind of speech, this speech 'trickles' and 'oozes' from him like a bodily fluid (Ellmann, 1982). By a further paradox the Catholic Church did provide manuals for use in the confessional which spelled out in considerable detail the various kinds of sexual 'sin' with which the confessor might have to deal and the appropriate penalties to be doled out. Stephen's confessor asks a series of discrete but pointed questions that seem to establish that Stephen's repeated acts of fornication in the Dublin brothels are the main cause of spiritual concern. However, he also confesses to his masturbation and it seems to be on the masturbation ('when that sin comes into your mind' *P*, 148) that the penance is based. Is the impact of this to return Stephen's sexual experiences to the more normal and venal range expected of a sixteen year old? Or, on the other hand, is masturbation taken by the priest to be the more serious transgression of a sexual code that justified the sex act only inasmuch as it was performed for reproductive purposes within marriage? On a symbolic plane, masturbation may most nearly approximate to the radical self-fathering transgressions of Stephen's new writerly apostasy, whose dangerously self-pleasuring, self-generating and self-legitimating aspects are clear.

HEAVENLY GOD!

As Stephen attempts to impose the gleaming new Loyolan system of personal organisation onto his daily life, new ramifications of the old antithesis between *physis* and *aesthesis* become apparent. The 'theatre' devoted to the human science of anatomy was the symbolic location of Stephen's self-development in the second chapter. Now mathematics is the tutelary discipline behind his conversion. Father Arnall has been recalled by some conscious or unconscious in the text from the Clongowes where he taught the boys 'hard sums', and such terms of reference as 'extension', 'intensity' and his graphic explanation of eternal duration have an obtrusively mathematical feel. Stephen has stared at a mathematical equation on his desk in the lead-up to the retreat. Aesthetically it transforms under his gaze into peacock feathers, eyes and stars but logically it intimates to him a Newtonian concept of error and correction, of chaos and order that he is already unable to obliterate as an analogy for his moral life. Bio-aesthetically his sexual and intellectual 'sin' is a truth to the body, but theolo-logically it is an 'error' whose ramifications are multiplied throughout the system into a Mandelbrot set of chaos:

It was his own soul going forth to experience, unfolding itself sin by sin, spreading abroad the balefire of its burning stars and folding back upon itself, fading slowly, quenching its own lights and fires. They were quenched: and the cold darkness filled chaos. (*P*, 106)

Chapter Four shows us a Stephen whose spiritual exercises are completely 'physical' in this precise sense that he has replaced aesthetics with a vision of the world as a divine 'theorem' and is obsessed by calculation: 'his soul in devotion pressing like fingers the keyboard of a great cash register' (*P*, 151). The absurdity of such bodily denial is exposed by Joyce's irony in such details as Stephen's 'anger at hearing his mother sneeze'. Spiritual 'ejaculations' and 'raptures' betray sensual undertones. His extraordinary series of sensual mortifications becomes an index of sensual experience. Confession is not a containment but a 'channel for the escape of scrofulous and unrepented imperfections' and his immersion in the erotic imagery of the *Song of Songs* shows that the repressive transvaluation is complete.

The seductions of perfection according to the priestly model are explored to the full, and Stephen's devotion eventually earns him one of the highest rewards that Belvedere can offer: an interview with the director where Stephen's ripeness for priestly vocation is explored. The scene is a small masterpiece of understatement where turbulent oceans of the unsaid wash through Stephen's brain as a decision about his true vocation gathers to a head. The director artfully comments on the various orders of monastic life regetting that: 'The capuchin dress, he thought, was rather too . . .'. His silence (assuming that Stephen might be put off by the femininity of the robes) and his reference to the French word '*jupes*' (leaving Stephen to consider the implications of the irreverent slang) spark off a blush (irreducibly human as Christopher Ricks in *Keats and Embarrassment* showed Darwin to have thought) whose 'tiny flame' conceals a train of complex erotic associations concerning women's underwear and Stephen's memories of his odd feelings of inadequacy as a Clongowes 'muff'.

Sharpening his attack, the director asks outright if he has a vocation, which almost gains an agreement from Stephen since, here as elsewhere, his mind is a fever of clearly heard and imagined inner voices. But in stressing the moral power and authority of the priestly office Conmee makes a tactical mistake since Stephen's ultra-moral self-interrogation dwells on the evil temptations of the power: the 'vague pomp' of its 'sacred offices'; its delicious jargons of 'tunicle', 'humeral veil', 'paten' and 'dalmatic cloth'. Above all the sexual psychology of the position intrigues him:

> He would know the sins, the sinful longings and sinful thoughts and sinful acts, of others, hearing them murmured into his ears in the confessional under the shame of a darkened chapel by the lips of women and of girls. (*P*, 162)

The mystical perfection of Melchisedec would render him an innocent reader of such texts, immune from their erotic subtext. Or would it? However hard he tries to repress them, his feelings remain and the priestly order feels 'chill' and repels him. His own pride and aloof shyness would be compromised by the submission to community but that is not the only social aspect of his choice.

At the end of the discussion he walks back home past 'a hamshaped encampment of poor cottages' huddled around 'the faded blue shrine of the Blessed Virgin' to what has now become an overcrowded kitchen, from which the Dedalus family are once again to be moved on. There in the messy kitchen where he can join with his brothers and sisters as they sing secular songs, he achieves his most generous and sympathetic social vision of 'the choirs of endless generations of children' and their legitimate, social '*hope of better things*' (*P*, 168). The implication may be that his ultimate choice of literary over priestly vocation is one which would allow an immersion in community that he could accept.

The climax of the fourth chapter has every claim to having lifted the poetic possibilities of prose in the novel to new heights, and raised its potential for psychological insight to new and as yet unsurpassed territory. No wonder that to some readers it has also seemed to be well over the top.

Stephen's vocational dialectic is resolved and the excitement and spiritual fullness of his choice of freedom over constraint sings with an extraordinary sensual and spiritual music, literally and metaphorically an imaginative flight or a 'fugue': 'leaping upwards a tone and downwards a diminished fourth'. As he strides along the harbour wall and beach, the landscape of Dublin, which has up to now been a labyrinth of small streets, opens up in all its maritime splendour to echo the excitements of his self-discovery. He cracks the bonds of duty that tie him to his father and the foetal bonds that have tied him to his mother. Calls of the figurative parents of Church and State can be outgrown.

He is not be a priest but is to go to university. He thrills with the Luciferian excitements of secular knowledge. A phrase from Hugh Miller's *Testament of the Rocks* seems to sum up his excitement with a reference to the sublime geological timescale that provided the Victorians with a scientific image of creation that overshadowed the myths of the Church. How appropriate it is that both Stephen and Joyce's university should have been the university of Newman's high-Victorian cultural idealism. Newman's curriculum was one of the first to include the study of English literature of which Joyce's texts have subsequently become so central a part.

So overwhelming is the sense of promise of great human achievement, intellectual freedom, knowledge and power that Stephen calls up another unconscious image of 'wild creatures racing, their feet pattering like rain upon the leaves' (*P*, 169). It is an image of legitimate wildness to exorcise his paralysing epiphany of hell in the last chapter and is conjured up by the magic of intertextuality from a punning bodily conundrum in Newman's own prose: '*Whose feet are as the feet of harts and underneath the everlasting arms*' (*P*, 169). Newman's odd phrase seems to stand as a representative of a whole range of contemporary turn-of-the-century New Age rhetorics from Alfred Orage to Havelock Ellis, Ibsen and Wilde.

In this high state of intellectual excitement everything becomes grist to the mill of his new aesthetic. He has discovered a new world, 'a new wild life', the America of the supposedly lower, so-called vegetable soul. Terms like 'soul', 'pride' and 'lust' (*P*, 174) can now be reglossed and revaluated as full and material terms in his aesthetic vocabulary. Having seized back language from the Jesuitical authorities that had usurped it, he can explore the true nature of his fascination with the surface of language. His is no mere empty interest in the 'colour' of words but a manipulation of their orders and rhythms by which he can create nothing less than an image of the unconscious mind; 'an inner world of individual emotions mirrored perfectly in a lucid supple periodic prose' (*P*, 171). The previously inhibiting coincidence of names and things now works on his side: his name calls up an image of the soaring mythic Daedalus and he even revels in its hidden promise that he might 'err' or 'fall' (*P*, 176). The language, by revaluing the 'ways of error' and sin and keying terms like 'heart' and 'wild', takes us by this punning coincidence back to the essay on Wilde with its diagnosis of 'sin' as the 'pulse' of art.

But the erotic organisation of Stephen's new aesthesis is not quite that of Wilde. In order to find the new empire of his soul he must first 'come out' as a heterosexual. Still dangerously overlyricised, the animal image of the bird/girl and her soft underwear provides a vital stage in the orientation of his aesthetic life. Her body and her 'quiet sufferance of his gaze, without shame or wantonness' offer the synthesis that Stephen's new life requires. A phrase culled from Joyce's cluttered 1904 sketch describing her as 'an envoy from the fair courts of life' is included, showing the consistency of the image in his literary/sexual ideal.

Sex and religion have been inverted and his repressions can be expressed. All he cries out is the single phrase 'Heavenly God!' As a divinity the bird-girl is a great improvement on the 'bovine god' (*P*, 115) he has escaped, but she is dangerously close to being another Pre-Raphaelite mystification. As a woman she is undefined and lacking in her own distinctive point of view; as a sexual object she remains merely distant and ideal. If *Dubliners* has provided us with images of repression, perhaps *A Portrait* deals rather with sublimation. It is the synthesis she offers for Stephen's psychodrama that most enthralls us. His search for a true opposite to the 'No' of priestly self-denial has not yet thrown up the 'Yes' of *Ulysses* so much as an ur-Beckettian 'on and on and on and on' (*P*, 176). In a territory where 'no word has broken the holy silence of his ecstasy' she is 'an angel of mortal youth and beauty' whose new world is a labial paradise, a body that speaks only itself, a text beyond language, promising endless erotic proliferations and enlightenments:

Glimmering and trembling, trembling and unfolding, a breaking light, an opening flower, it spread in endless succession to itself, breaking in full crimson and unfolding and fading to palest rose, leaf by leaf and wave of light by wave of light. (*P*, 177)

LITERARY THEORY

The university that is the setting for the final chapter of *A Portrait* differs in some degree from the ideal – imaged as a half-naked girl on a beach in the mind of an Edwardian sixth-former – that we have glimpsed. Is Joyce's intention merely to deflate Stephen? What may underpin the mental conflict at the level of character is a discursive rupture within the politics and ideology of cultural knowledge itself. Stephen's new life may be lyricised and idealised in the expansive discourses of high-Victorian liberalism, but seen through the reducing lens of 'realism' (with its roots in the discourses of eighteenth-century political economy), there is only the image of 'a box of pawn tickets' to show.

In the 'economic' terms of this kind of realism Stephen's victory for subjective over Loyolan devotional time is imaged as little more than a luxurious absent-mindedness and a tendency to be late for lectures. The resolution of Stephen's vocational dialectic leaves him trying to 'forge out an esthetic philosophy' which may issue in artistic production while also needing to serve as a kind of private self-assertion against the discursive pressures that are put upon him from outside. During the final chapter he manages to produce one piece of self-confessed poetic 'drivel' and another more amibitious poem: the ornate and opaque Pre-Raphaelite villanelle which the text compels us to read. He also keeps a diary and its thoughts and notes as well as the richness of his mental associations throughout the chapter are far more poetic than the poems themselves. His thoughts being in the usual sense private, the discursive form that offers the most complete expression of his new aesthesis of images of women, of the 'wet branches' of 'rainladen trees', of Elizabethan lyrics and so on is literary theory. In no sense do the lectures he attends in English ('dates of birth or death, chief works, a favourable and an unfavourable criticism side by side') respond to his appetite for aesthesis. Indeed the only lecture that we see Stephen attending at length is a physics lecture, whose obscene bodily subtext is revealed by student heckling and calls. Once more the old distinction between physis and aesthesis is brought to mind.

Stephen's ideas seem no more able than student obscenity to break out into the public discursive world. His New Age rhetoric has been hijacked by student political voices that leave him no less isolated than before. MacCann, for instance, is not so 'antisocial' as Stephen, he will 'work and act' for 'social liberty and equality among all classes and sexes in the United States of the Europe of the future' (*P*, 181). Davin's 'peasant' innocence, his Gaelic League enthusiasm for myth and Irish field-sports and his little vignette of the peasant woman's sexual offer seems honest and 'homely' beside Stephen's deep fears of disloyalty and betrayal.

The Dean of Studies and his office fire call up the 'useful' as opposed to Stephen's ideal and self-legitimating forms of knowledge that are described as 'like looking down from the Cliffs of Moher into the depths' (*P*, 191). To the Dean, Stephen, for all his intellectual posturing, is just another slightly delinquent student. No less than the shadowy 'Moonan' to whom he is compared, Stephen may 'perish of inanition'. Even the primeval chaos of fire is put to domestic use by the Dean. His term for 'funnel' (beyond the nationalist issue raised by MacCabe and Seamus Heaney) names the object according to its use value; Stephen's term 'tundish' implies an aesthetic apprehension of the shape of the thing in itself. Freedom, defined as an unexploited sense of difference, would be a threat to his mentality but is not to Stephen's aesthetic absolutism, according to which 'there is no such thing as freedom' since 'all thinking is bound by its own laws' (*P*, 191).

Difference is a key term of Stephen's emerging consciousness: a difference whose outward sign is difference in language. 'How different' he observes, 'are the words *home, Christ, ale, Master*, on his lips and on mine!': four key words (like the four last things of the sermons) that hint at an eschatology of difference. The terms throw out an interesting network of associations with ideas of authority and escape, but only 'home' (or 'homely') has actually been used by the Dean in the conversation that we have heard. It calls up Stephen's collapsing, shifting family home and his desire to escape from all the 'nets' of feeling and idea that trap him there and prevent him from improving its lot. We remember the occurrence of the word in the mind of Eveline in *Dubliners* or in Freud's essay on the *unheimlich* that helps us to understand the subtext of sexual repression in 'The Dead'. Something is also in danger of being repressed in the 'reality' of Stephen's university, whose subtly communicated cloistered atmosphere we might relate historically to the retention of an element of moral instruction in Newman's limited ideal. Neither Davin's 'homely' Irishness nor the Dean's praise of the 'homely' metaphor of Epictetus's lamp seems right to Stephen's questioning mind. 'What lay behind it or within it?' he asks and he calls up a counter-association in Epictetus's image of the soul as 'a bucketful of water' whose subtext in Joyce's own pseudo-Freudian iconoclasm we can trace to an angry letter he wrote to his brother in 1906 about the 'syphilitic' 'sexual department' of the soul (*SL*, 129).

Ireland and Church are 'home' neither to Stephen nor to the Dean. Stephen traces the thread of the Dean's conversion 'winding up to the end like a reel of cotton some finespun reasoning' back to a variety of ultra-Protestant sects: 'six principle men, peculiar people, seed and snake baptists, supralapsarian dogmatists' (*P*, 193). Like Ariadne's thread it may provide Stephen with a means of intellectual escape, marking out a route from the very Protestant sense of the 'peculiar' to the sense of 'difference' that opens up the cultural territory that is to be Stephen's own.

The discursive territory of culture, which is neither sex, politics nor religion but includes all three, offers Stephen his route for ideological escape. In order to found his new discourse he must have an audience but there is much competition for the discursive space, starting with MacCann's offer of 'universal peace' to which even the 'tame goose' nationalist Davin is, despite his paramilitary leanings, prepared to subscribe. The 'gypsy student' Temple has a humanistic loyalty that allows him a fleeting confederacy with Stephen and his closest personal friend Cranly, but Cranly's down-to-earth good sense (he thinks of him as a 'bleating goat') sees him off. Davin's accusation that he is a 'sneerer' provokes Stephen's anxiety that Irish nationalism is a history of betrayals. He is disturbingly serious in his beliefs, and while Cranly and Davin are content to play handball, Stephen takes Lynch aside and, despite his protests, subjects him to a lengthy lecture on his theory of art.

Distinguishing between 'pity' and 'terror' (on the grounds that the one shows us the sufferer, the other the cause of suffering, he speeds on to a subsidiary distinction between proper and improper arts (on the grounds that the latter do not arouse 'loathing' or 'desire'). This might seem to be an ascetic rather than an aesthetic theory and it is no wonder that Lynch heckles with telling references to the statues of Venus in the National Museum as he proceeds to define a semi-mystical perception of objects as separate in themselves and divisible into all their parts, a mystic state to which the artist himself conforms as he ascends from the emotional 'lyrical' form to the transcendent and godlike 'dramatic' form in which his personality is refined out of existence (*P*, 219). His theory, as he freely admits, is a reader-oriented one of 'apprehension' and Lynch looks forward eagerly to the more substantial 'phenomena of artistic conception artistic gestation and artistic reproduction' that will require a new – apparently more biological than metaphysical – terminology and some long overdue 'new personal experience'. Stephen's theory is not really a theory of something; it is that something itself. The interruption of Donovan meanwhile shows the final-year students to have passed their exams and to be going off to the world of work to which neither Lynch nor Stephen can as yet aspire.

Stephen's theorising is bogged down in the terminolgy of his Jesuit education as his absurd list of scholastic questions (echoing the earlier questions of school teachers) ironically suggests. It would be absurd to relate the sophisticated aesthetic sensitivity that produced such a knowing psychological and social portrait as that of Stephen with the first pale efforts of Stephen himself. Joyce's book was written with the experience of clopement and economic struggle, of battling with the censor, of his letters to Nora, and the collapse of European liberal consensus behind him, which for Stephen are still only in prospect.

Stephen tries to relate aesthetic to sexual beauty and in so doing provides a distinction between reproduction and eroticism that is a useful analogy for the distinction between a utilitarian (pornographic and didactic) and a true art. But what finally reduces him to a welcome silence is the merest glimpse of E—C— whom he feels (though he seems hardly to know her and we are unclear from his memories whether he has even seen her for eight years) – like Ireland – to have been guilty of some form of betrayal.

Compared to the prose that surrounds it the poem that he writes in the next episode is a disappointment – at least as a vehicle for expressing the complex feelings and associations that might make up the desire to write a poem. Once again the poem is presented in the context of the memories and associations that produced it, and once again it is as a kind of sexual compensation that it is best understood. If the stories in

Dubliners tell of repression, then nothing in *A Portrait* so clearly as
this poem tells of sublimation. The repetitions of its villanelle form
suggest a dialectic but it is an unresolved dialectic with no progress
into a third term.

The process of composition denies the asceticism of the theory
since the poem's creativity is clearly said to result from a 'glow of
desire'. Little, even in the highly aesthetic lyrics that Joyce himself
composed when he was a student, might prepare us for the 'inanition'
and aestheticism of this poem.

Its pure belief in literature as the 'highest and most spiritual art' sits
in stark contrast to the moralistic heckling of the audience for the
opening night of the Irish National Theatre that we briefly glimpse in
this chapter. As Stephen continues to muse on the high-flown literary
culture of the Renaissance – lines from Dowland and Nashe – that
both aesthetes and modernists constructed as a time of lost national
and spiritual unity, the world around is one of increasingly intense
student political debate or cynicism, local poverty and disfigurement.

The penultimate section of the book locks Stephen in a long
discusssion with Cranly, who has emerged as his closest confidant and
secular 'confessor'. The position Stephen adopts is even more than
usually proud and selfish and many readers will feel more sympathy
with the good sense of Cranly, who urges Stephen to compromise in
his atheism at least for his mother's sake and to give up his absurd
attachment to 'ideas'. Cranly's conversation brings out some of the
hidden social realities about his family life (his mother's 'nine or ten'
children) that Stephen cannot normally reveal. Stephen admits his
desire for and disbelief in finding a 'Rosie O'Grady' to match the
romantic ideals of popular culture, while for Cranly – superficially at
least – she would be easy to find. The debate becomes another piece of
casuistry about moral freedom: what it is that Stephen is prepared to
do; what crimes he would be prepared to commit. Much in Cranly's
questioning implies that he has a maturity and understanding that
Stephen lacks, but Stephen's desire for freedom is nothing like the
image of experimental criminality proposed by Cranly. It consists in
his desire to live out his own fate in Brunonian or Ibsenite terms. His
formula of 'silence, exile and cunning' may be the watchword of a
new aesthetic but may also, more disturbingly, be nothing more than a
codification of the everyday morality that pretends to be something
else.

Stephen holds up the image of his own mind, thoughts and feelings against the spiritual authorities of the Catholic Church, but, as he is all too aware, that mind may itself be not only capable of, but perhaps characterised by error. This seems to be the recognition of the sequence of ideas sparked off by a line from Nashe 'Darkness falls from the air', which, it turns out, he has misread or remembered wrongly (*P*, 237–8). Error, imaged as the louse on his neck that is produced by his own thoughts, is the condition to which he willingly consigns himself. An Othello-like jealousy infects his mind. The search for absolutes, brought on by his sceptical turn of mind and his determination to read all signs as signs and omens appropriate to his own fate, lead him into a disastrous sexual situation. All he can stand is the most fleeting glimpse of E—C— and then the mere fact of her glancing at Cranly and of Cranly's blush is enough to set off a trail of speculations that lead ultimately to his willing renunciation of her for 'some clean athlete who washed himself every morning' before he has even given her his own best shot.

The jealous anxieties that let loose the sexual torrent of Joyce's 1909 letters, the theme of *Exiles* and the central situation of *Ulysses* are all glimpsed here. So is the theme of Stephen as reader or interpreter, who has now got himself into a situation where he interprets everything as a personal slight. Cranly's final comment about his need to be alone he interprets as – and ultimately turns into – the end of their friendship.

The beautiful augury of the birds at the start of Section Three is to be confirmed by the ending. All that is now left open to Stephen is departure, and while Joyce's own flight in 1904 was a rather more hopeful elopement with the Nora whose physical immediacy had evidently found some way of getting behind Joyce's defences, Joyce leaves his Stephen without a mate. The final diary form is in that sense both a triumph and tragedy of his self-creation, which the diary form itself can be said to echo. Who reads a diary? For Tindall (1959) the diary form that ends the book is the form 'of a man in love with himself'. Perhaps so. But for the intellectual thread in Stephen's story of self-development it represents a fitting conclusion. No form more suits the sceptic turn of mind that vindicates feelings and experience only through the detail of a stylishly crafted fragment. No form more easily enables the idiosyncratic trains of association and idea that are the truest and best products of Stephen's mind to be recorded. No form more effectively resists the narrative closure of traditional romance.

The atmosphere of spring, the glimpses of the girl and of Cranly, the calling-up of ghosts, the lively images, dreams and speculations need no other justification than that they are what Stephen thought and felt. The diary is filled with the sense of purpose and excitement, of the absolute rightness of rejecting national rebellion and priestly domination for a cosmopolitan attachment to 'culture' that one also feels in the letters Joyce wrote home, despite financial hardships, in the period 1904–8. Free from the shackles of constrained time and from a Yeatsian sense of tradition, Stephen is committed to the future of 'the loveliness that has not yet come into the world' and thoroughly opposed to the cowardly ignorance of the Irish around him represented by the Mulrennan (who could be a character from Synge or O'Casey) who fears the 'terrible queer creatures at the latter end of the world' (*P*, 256).

Stephen's apostasy is a success, though its implied romantic subtext would leave Stephen in a postion of ridiculous failure before E—C— 'like a fellow throwing a handful of peas into the air'. This, though, the reader may be invited to see as a temporary situation. Stephen's final 'Welcome' to 'life', and his determination to learn 'what the heart is and what it feels' returns us to the true core of his aesthetic idealism: its hunger for a literary and sexual space that can be discovered beyond the Jesuitical territorialisation of his mind; its sympathy for the social trials (if not the ideological loyalties) of the brothers and sisters of his family; its attempts to breach the Cartesian divide that still too narrowly intellectualises his literary-theoretical ideas.

Odd as it may seem, the reader may not only approve but applaud his ambition to 'forge in the smithy of my soul the uncreated conscience of may race' while still retaining a hope that such an extraordinary goal may be – indeed may already have begun to be – accomplished.

READING LIST

Wayne Booth, *The Rhetoric of Fiction*, 2nd edn (Chicago: University of Chicago Press, 1983) pp. 323–36.

Kenneth Burke, 'Fact, Inference and Proof in the Analysis of Literary Symbolism', in *Terms for Order*, ed. Stanley Hyman (Bloomington: Indiana University Press, 1964) pp. 145–72.

Christopher Butler, 'Joyce and the Displaced Author', in *James Joyce and Modern Literature*, ed. W. J. McCormack and A. Stead (London: Routledge, 1984) pp. 56–73.

Joseph A. Buttigeig, *A Portrait of the Artist in Different Perspective* (Athens: Ohio University Press, 1987).

Terry Eagleton, *Exiles and Emigrés* (London: Chatto, 1965).

Terry Eagleton, *The Ideology of the Aesthetic* (Oxford: Blackwell, 1990).

Maud Ellmann, 'Polytropic Man', in *James Joyce: New Perspectives*, ed. Colin MacCabe (Brighton: Harvester, 1982) pp. 73–103.

Edmund Epstein, *The Ordeal of Stephen Dedalus* (Carbondale: Southern Illinois University Press, 1971).

Karen Lawrence, 'Gender and Narrative Voice in *Jacob's Room* and *A Portrait of the Artist as a Young Man*', in *James Joyce: The Centennial Symposium*, ed. M. Beja *et al.* (Urbana: University of Illinois Press, 1986).

Roy Pascal, 'The Autobiographical Novel and Autobiography', *Essays in Criticism*, 9 (1959) pp. 134–50.

Jean-Michel Rabaté, *James Joyce: Authorized Reader* (Baltimore: Johns Hopkins University Press, 1991).

John Paul Riquelme, 'A Portrait of the Artist as a Young Man', in *The Cambridge Companion to James Joyce*, ed. D. Attridge (Cambridge: Cambridge University Press, 1989).

Dorothy van Ghent, *Form and Function in the English Novel* (New York: Viking, 1959) pp. 263–76.

3

Ulysses

BEGINNINGS

It was in Rome in 1906 that Joyce first thought of the idea of writing a story for *Dubliners* called 'Ulysses' based on a man called Hunter who was Jewish and whose wife was rumoured to have been sexually unfaithful (Ellmann, 1982). It is just possible to imagine the story fitting into the collection as another tale of repressed bourgeois sexuality, but by the time Joyce got down to work on it in Zurich in 1914, extraordinary possibilities for a kind of exponential literary growth from this small germ had become apparent.

The title – evidently ironic – opened up an exploration of epic, mock-heroic and parodic possibilties that seemed to take half of European cultural history into account. Joyce researched extravagantly, exploring anything from nineteenth-century scholarly debates about the precise geographical location of Odysseus's voyages (Groden, 1980) to an obscure little comic poem by one Frank Hopewell published in Dublin in 1741 called 'The Oddity', written as 'a sailor's farewell to his sweetheart' with all its lines rhyming on '-ation' (Brown, 1985).

In terms of the prevalent cultural stereotypes of the period, the idea of a Jewish protagonist might have seemed an opportunity for an attack on bourgeois marital avariciousness, with a Jewish 'Ulysses' throwing up all kinds of potential for comic indulgence. But Joyce's distaste for the racial stereotypings of contemporary Irish nationalism was very strong and his drift from Christianity (not to mention his sexual encounters with Jewish women) made him highly sympathetic to Jews as intrinsic social marginals within Christian society and as carriers of an alternative pre- or non-Christian humanity. Rather than

stereotyping Jews as 'other', his identification with a part-Jewish protagonist gave Joyce the more exciting potential for a radical critical
distance from the racial assumptions of contemporary Irish nationalist
rhetoric.

Before the First World War the idea of 'race' was a rallying cry of
idealistic and anti-imperial new forces within Europe, and it was a sufficiently fluid and metaphorical term for Stephen Dedalus in launching
his exile to declare his intention to be that of forming 'the uncreated
conscience of his race'. By the Second World War 'race' had become
the dirtiest four-letter word in Europe and Joyce's invention of a
mixed racial character for his epic of Christo-Judaic secularism and
European modernity was both a diagnosis and a potential cure for the
disease, offering a cultural mixture that might deconstruct many of the
deep-rooted cultural assumptions of everyday life.

The theme of the cuckold – a traditional subject for comic and
grotesque treatment – had already been used as an intimate window
into the psychology of Gabriel Conroy in 'The Dead'. Conroy's experience of being decentred in his wife's affections is deeply linked to
Stephen's feelings of being undervalued by E—C— in *A Portrait* and
to Joyce's own anxieties about Nora's fidelity. Declaring even Shakespeare's *Othello* to be an inadequate treatment, he wrote *Exiles* where
Rowan's response to the possibility of his wife having an affair is
elaborated into a kind of moral test for his non-possessive sexual
avant-gardism. Some critics have interpreted the exaggerated and
intellectualised austerity of these husbandly stances – which almost
amount to a sexual offer of the partner to other males – as an unconscious form of male-bonding or homosexuality (Empson, 1991) or as
masochism (Henke, 1990). Seamus Deane suggests that Joyce's fears
were also tied to his rejection of – prompted by fears of betrayal by –
Irish political and Catholic faiths. But in *Exiles* Richard's austere
'living wounding' doubt seems to be offered as no less than a paradigm of the modern intellectual situation. In the morality of Joyce's
time such transgressions of strict marital legitimacy opened up the
potential for an exploration of the whole transgressive territory of conscious and unconscious sexual life, as rich, if not richer than more
recent treatments from Pinter's *Betrayal* to Julian Barnes's *Before She
Met Me*.

To this already complex mixture of ideas and associations Joyce
discovered at an early stage that he could add a kind of sequel to *A*

Portrait of the Artist with Stephen Dedalus returned to Dublin for his mother's funeral but still determined not to succumb to her faith. This sequel would give Joyce the opportunity to chart the development of his literary theory still further and once again to provide within the text itself a model, surrogate or emblem of the heroically brilliant kind of reader that such a book would inevitably demand.

By this time Joyce's own thinking on aesthetic questions had developed a long way from the brief notes from Aquinas jotted down in a notebook in 1903 that he had used to construct Stephen for *A Portrait*. He was now over thirty, a father, lecturing on *Hamlet* to a sophisticated post-Freudian audience in Trieste. His lecture notes show him wielding advanced tools of critical interpretation: Dover Wilson's archaeology of Elizabethan social and theatrical contexts; biographies by Frank Harris and Sidney Lee; the post-Ibsenite criticism of Georg Brandes. Joyce noted down Voltaire's idea of the plays as the 'fruit of the imagination of a drunken savage' suggesting how far European neo-classicism could come to accounting for Shakespearean totality (Quillian, 1978).

The postcard on which Joyce first mentioned the resumed project – written in German from Zurich to his brother in gaol in Trieste – reveals the European wartime context and the linguistic mixedness of the book: '*Die erste Episode meines neues Roman "Ulysses" ist geschrieben*' (*SL*, 209). Episodic construction, which had already been used in 'The Dead' and in *A Portrait*, was to become the guiding mechanism of an unprecedentedly episodic book. 'I am doing it', he wrote to Pound in 1917, 'by different means in different parts' (attributing to Aristotle such an un-Aristotelian idea), and the postcard shows that 'the Hamlet chapter' (in which Stephen's theory of the play is clearly based on Joyce's lectures) was one of the first to be completed, or at least complete enough to consider sending on (*SL*, 225).

As the project burgeoned over the next years into a work as long as the longest 24-episode, multi-volume Victorian novel but twice as various and compacted, the relatively straightforward narrative of the opening sections gave way to the explosive stylistic extravaganza of the book's second half. Joyce was by now supported by the generosity of Harriet Shaw Weaver, once editor and now publisher of the *Egoist* magazine in which *A Portrait* had been serialised in England. By the time he had completed the eleventh or 'Sirens' episode in 1919, in which the writing plays decorative musical tricks with itself, he was having to apologise to her. The multiplicity of methods adopted was too complex to be easily explained and yet was 'like the progress of some sandblast' through artistic culture (*SL*, 240–1).

As the pace and scale of technical innovation grew, so the process of writing became a process of rewriting. Nowhere was this more apparent than in the way in which the seventh episode, 'Aeolus', was rewritten as late as 1921 to incorporate a series of parodic newspaper-like headings and a variety of formal rhetorical tropes that cannibalise its narrative norm. Karen Lawrence focuses on this moment in the stylistic amplification of the book but the expansion was not merely stylistic. More and more extravagant and obscene material was being accumulated as if to subvert aesthetic notions of civility and decorum with new ideals of inclusive grotesquery and excess. The contemporary liberal critic Havelock Ellis proposed an etymology of the 'obscene' as meaning 'off the scene'. In *Ulysses* what would normally be excluded is included, and what would normally be repressed is expressed, and in this sense the book might be defined as triumphantly and heroically – Gargantuanly – obscene.

Moralities and ideologies are of necessity 'offended' by this kind of writing. So are the more literary confines and boundaries of genre. One of the most recurring of critical problems has been to try to define the genre of the book (Litz, 1974) and Joyce himself, having begun with '*Roman*' soon found himself having to invent terms like '*Homerischen ungeheuer*' and '*maledetissimo romanzaccione*', or simply rely on 'book'. Though the novel itself is that genre of writing which may be defined by its very novelty, *Ulysses* began to defy containment even by that term. Joyce wrote

It is the epic of two races (Israel–Ireland) and at the same time the cycle of the human body as well as a little story of a day (life). It is also a kind of encyclopaedia. My intention is not only to render the myth *sub specie tempus nostri* but also to allow each adventure (that is, every hour, every organ, every art being interconnected and interrelated in the somatic scheme of the whole) to condition and even to create its own technique. (*SL*, 271)

The book had become an extraordinary mixture of different parts that defied even authorial containment and could only be said to be writing themselves. Translating Joyce himself from Irish exile and

Text continues on p. 68

1 *Ulysses*: simplified structural chart

No.	Place	Time	Principal character	Narrative Base	Figures	Homeric name
				I: The Telemachiad		
1	Breakfast 1: the tower	8	Stephen	3rd person and inner monologue	Adverbs	Telemachus
2	Deasy's school	10	Stephen	3rd person inner m.		Nestor
3	The beach	11	Stephen	Inner m.		Proteus
				II: The Adventures		
4	Breakfast 2: 7 Eccles St.	8	Bloom (Molly)	3rd person inner m.		Calypso
5	Streets, bath	10	Bloom	3rd person inner m.		Lotus Eaters
6	Funeral of Dignam	11	Bloom (Stephen)	3rd person inner m. *		Hades
7	Newspaper office	12	Bloom Stephen	3rd person 2 inner m.	Headlines Figures	Aeolus
8	Streets, lunch	1	Bloom	3rd person inner m.		Lestry-gonians
9	Library	2	Stephen (Bloom) *	3rd person inner m. *	Inner dialogue	Scylla and Charybdis
10	Streets	3	Several *	3rd person 4 inner m. *	Perspective Insertions	Wandering Rocks
11	Ormond Hotel	4	Bloom	3rd person inner m.	Musical form	Sirens
12	Barney Kiernan's	5	Bloom	1st person	Parodic insertions	Cyclops
13	The beach	8	Bloom	3rd person + inner m.	Parody (half)	Nausicaa
14	Maternity hospital	10	Bloom Stephen	3rd person	Sequence of parodies	Oxen of the Sun
15	Brothel district	12	Bloom Stephen	Drama	Hallucin-ation	Circe
				III: The Homecoming		
16	Cabmens' shelter	1	Bloom Stephen	3rd person	Redund-ancy	Eumaeus
17	7 Eccles St.: kitchen	2	Bloom Stephen	3rd person	Question and answer	Ithaca
18	Bedroom	None	Molly	Inner m.	Body words no punctu-ation	Penelope

Notes to Chart

Most readers of *Ulysses* begin by making or relying on some such scheme as this, not least among the interests of which are the inevitable points and anomalies which arise.

1. *Points of division* Joyce wrote *Ulysses* in eighteen untitled chapters or episodes divided into three numbered sections, given as I, II and III above. Subsequent readers have used the familiar Homeric titles for each chapter, which Joyce himself used during the process of composition. Different critics have adopted different strategies for describing its structural patterns. Ellmann (1972) divides it into six triads. Others, including Kenner (1980) and MacCabe (1978) see two halves, with the break occuring either before or after episode 10, when the technical virtuosity of the book accelerates. For Karen Lawrence the book's 'second half' begins with episode 7. My divisions attempt to represent these and other possibilities. It may be worth noting that a glance at the otherwise tight time scheme reveals large gaps between episodes 12 and 13, 13 and 14 and 14 and 15. These also contribute to a sense of the structural pattern of the whole.

2. *Principal characters* However obscured or belittled they are by their circumstances and by the narrative strategy, we may say that Stephen is the principal character in four episodes (1, 2, 3, 9), Bloom in seven (4, 5, 6, 8, 11, 12, 13) and Molly in one (18). In five further episodes (7, 14, 15, 16, 17) neither Stephen nor Bloom predominates. In episode 10 their importance is levelled to that of several other 'background' characters. Where principal characters are glimpsed in episodes where another predominates I have indicated this in parenthesis.

3. *Narrative base and figure* The notes given here do not follow exactly the terms for the technique of each episode given by Joyce himself (see Ellmann, 1972) but attempt to provide a brief indication of the most obvious stylistic features of the episode for a new reader approaching the text with conventional narrative assumptions. Joyce's 'third-person' narrative is never merely conventional and has been much discussed (see Kenner, Lawrence, Hayman and so on). I use the term 'inner dialogue' to distinguish those features occurring in episode 9 (though by no means exclusive to it) whereby both Stephen's monologue and the narrative voice are given the character of dialogue. It should be added that at least some element of the manner of each episode can be discovered in several of the others.

4. *Order of composition and publication* Joyce probably drafted episodes 1–3 and 16 in Trieste before 1914. In Zurich, between 1914 and 1919 he drafted to a near complete state episodes 4–12, having nearly completed episode 9 by 1916. Episodes 13 and 14 were substantially written in Trieste in the first half of 1920. In Paris between the summers of 1920 and 1921, he composed episodes 15, 17 and 18 and revised 16. As with episode 7, recast in October 1921, he thoroughly revised and expanded earlier episodes in the light of later developments before publication in 1922. Serial publication in the *Little Review* (Chicago) of episodes 1–14 began in March 1918 and was stopped in September 1920. In England extracts from four chapters appeared in *The Egoist* between January and December 1919.

obscurity to the pinnacle of European cultural centrality, its compositional process of self-cannibalisation embodied that translation. Through inclusion and revision it becomes a book to end all books: at once seeming to chew up and spit out past literatures, but in another sense preserving everything it negates and thereby saving the literary word for the post-literate world.

Joyce made a suggestive sketch of a Chaplinesque Bloom and wrote above it the first line of Homer's *Odyssey* whose Greek term for Odysseus is 'polytropos', familiar to English readers as the 'man of many ways'. Joyce's gloss unprecedentedly puns with the idea of a rhetorical or novelistic 'trope' to unlock the potential for an unprecedentedly polytropic book. The chaotic and licentious inclusiveness of such a project is, according to some Brunonian logic of coinciding contraries, at one and the same time a massive act of reordering on the strictest formal principles. Focused through Dublin's turbulent microcosm, it is European culture broken down and reconsituted before during and after the First World War.

Nobody now denies the definitive greatness of Joyce's achievement in *Ulysses*. It would be hard to find a post-Joycean writer in the language who, whether by imitation or reaction, has escaped his influence. Only the numbing reverential aura born of that very centrality and authority is now likely to threaten or frustrate the reader of Joyce.

Critical and academic reception was, however slow to warm in certain quarters. In England, in particular, the sense among F. R. Leavis and many of his followers that *Ulysses* lacked a unity of vision and coherence was influential for many years. The native Lawrence was preferred as a celebrant of social mobility through cultural education, as novelist of the Oedipal family and of sexual liberalism. Much English criticism has been influenced by European social traditions of thought, and traditional Lukácsian preferences for narrative realism over Modernism also led until recently to guarded or ambivalent attitudes to Joyce among such English socialist critics from Alick West in the 1930s to Arnold Kettle in the 1960s.

In the 1930s Stuart Gilbert (1952, p. 40) defended Joyce's place not in the English but the European 'great tradition' which 'begins with

Homer' and in the 1950s Richard Ellmann's massive biography fully recuperated Joyce for academic humanist criticism. When the absolute rule of liberal humanist values in criticism came to be questioned in the late 1960s and 1970s and the narrow economies of Leavisite critical discourse were expanded, features of Joyce's work (its post-culturalism and post-literacy, its obscenity, its radical perspectivism, its stylistic encyclopaedia and genetic turmoil) that had at first presented difficulties themselves became central justifications for the continued study of his work.

In Britain, through the work of mainstream British social or culturalist critics such as Raymond Williams and Terry Eagleton (as much as through the American academic Joyce industry) *Ulysses* began to be recentralised both as a tragedy of modern urban alienation and as the most 'social' of novels: the great novel of the artist in the city and the first fictional intimation of economic consumerism, investigating in its very texture the complex interrelation of economic and psychological life.

Feminist ideology found in *Ulysses* both a territory for the exposure and indictment of modern bourgeois hetero-homosexual norms and stereotypes and radical possibilities for their subversion and renewal. Narrow feminist rejections like that of Sandra Gilbert (1988) have been amply balanced by the brilliant speculations about female language made by Kristeva and Cixous (Johnson, 1989).

The increasing dependence on language and linguistic theory in academic discussion further encouraged the centralising of Joyce since critics like David Lodge and younger theorists such as Colin MacCabe, Stephen Heath, Maud Ellmann and Derek Attridge have made Joyce's texts a central platform for their work. Even the deconstruction of the concept of 'authority' has led some to argue for the 're-authorisation' of the very critiques of authority embodied in Joyce's texts (Mahaffey, 1986).

Over the past thirty years academic study of narrative has gradually become more 'scientific', more 'narratological'. With its extravagantly performed exercises in narrative style and technique, *Ulysses* has provided a focus for such study and offers itself as an encyclopaedia of narrative technique. As an exemplary English academic critic of narrative of the post-war generation, Barbara Hardy shows a typical development: having relegated *Ulysses* in 1964 to the margins of *The Appropriate Form* she reasserted its centrality in *Tellers and Listeners* in 1975 as an encyclopaedic repository of narratives and narrative forms.

Under an Orwellian stylistic economy much British fiction of the 1950s respected Joyce but left his example to the idealised margins of literary practice, to Beckett or to the poetically based prose of writers like Dylan Thomas from the Celtic fringe. Writers like Kingsley Amis and Iris Murdoch, or even William Golding, seemed to function within the narrative expectations that *Ulysses* had overturned. In the 1960s and 1970s the experimentations of Fowles, and the explicitly Joycean attempts of writers like Anthony Burgess and B. S. Johnson to form alternative kinds of 'snotgreen gannetspath' (linking Joycean and Anglo-Saxon traditions) have been well to the fore. Examples, from the 'tolerably spermy and Joycean' Charles Highway of Martin Amis's *The Rachel Papers* to the magisterial post-cultural reconstructivism of A. S. Byatt's *Possession* and the heroic post-Joycean multicultural secularism of Salman Rushdie, suggest that the Joycean example is no less alive in contemporary British fiction than in any other fiction of today.

ART IN THE AGE OF MECHANICAL REPRODUCTION

As if we were reading two different newspaper reports of the same day's events, 16 June 1904, the great day of *Ulysses* has two beginnings: one for Stephen and one for Bloom as they take their respective breakfasts at 8 o'clock and begin their respective days. Like all city dwellers they may be related by any number of seen or unseen filiations but are also apart: divided by age, by religious background, by occupation, by complexities of social class.

Stephen is a brilliant graduate, half-employed as a part-time teacher, partly a vindication but also partly an endictment of Newman's elevated cultural and educational ideal. He nurses huge intellectual ambitions but in social terms he is the drifting and disengaged victim of his peers and associates. His promised triumph in exile has failed to materialise. He has returned to Dublin for his mother's funeral but he will not be reconciled to her creed and is haunted by her image.

His day begins with a shaving scene whose antics and mockery locate the book as parody and as a bodily rewriting of religious ritual from the start. They breakfast at the coastline tower that Stephen and ebullient medical student Buck Mulligan inhabit with the visiting English cultural tourist Haines – a Romantic affectation that none of them can really afford. Stephen goes on to teach a lesson in classical history in the local school but he barely keeps his pupils' attention since his mind is a ferment of self-generating and self-legitimating associations and ideas. His intellectual victory is, perhaps, like that of Pyrrhus whose story he teaches and whose legacy the Dublin boys translate: '*Another victory like that and we are done for.*' He is, however, useful to the school headmaster who gives him a letter to take off to the Dublin papers where he is known to the editors.

His true brilliance and potential only emerge in the sustained inner monologue that accompanies his walk along the beach into the centre of Dublin. In this extraordinary mental poetry his past life and anxieties merge with philosophical and artistic speculations, laying down a tissue of associations that prefigures the rest of his day's experiences. Its best theme (and another key to the whole book) is summed up in its opening phrases 'the ineluctable modality of the visible' and 'Signatures of all things I am here to read.' Stephen's role as a surrogate for the reader-as-hero, who here begins to get an intimation of some of the demands *Ulysses* is to make, is apparent in these phrases. The nineteenth-century Carlylean artist-hero is transformed into the post-culturalist reader-hero. To readers familiar with Roland Barthes's distinction between writerly (*scriptible*) and readerly (*lisible*) texts, it is the 'ineluctable modality of the *lisible*' that is here proclaimed. Yet for some readers Stephen is still a failure, managing to produce in the public sense from this extraordinary cerebration only one single verse stanza, about a vampire, parodying a love song in the female voice by the Romantic poet Douglas Hyde, which he scribbles on a torn-off corner of Deasy's letter on the foot-and-mouth disease.

The intellectual decorum of the second breakfast at the Bloom household in Eccles Street is quite antithetical to this. In Stephen's mind there is Aristotle; in Bloom's kidneys. Once again the reader may be made aware of the importance of the physical body, Bloom's organs directing his or her attention to the structural principle connecting each episode to an organ of the body, making *Ulysses* the most *organ*-ised of books.

The introduction of Bloom at the start of this fourth episode is one of literature's triumphs in the depiction of ordinary everydayness, but the technique is far from ordinary, gradually easing the reader from the third-person descriptions of an implied narrator to the direct transcription of Bloom's thoughts and associations that is the substance of interior monologue. The contents and rhythms of Bloom's curiosities and associations feel quite different from Stephen's thoughts, though the syntactic shapes of their monologues are more similar than might first appear.

Here, from the second episode, is an example of Stephen as he both vividly and morbidly remembers his reading of Aristotle in a Paris library:

> Fed and feeding brains about me: under glowlamps, impaled, with faintly beating feelers: and in my mind's darkness a sloth of the underworld, reluctant, shy of brightness, shifting her dragon scaly folds. Thought is the thought of thought. Tranquil brightness. The soul is in a manner all that is: the soul is the form of forms. Tranquility sudden, vast, candescent: form of forms. (*U*, 21)

Similar syntactic breakages produce vastly different effects in this passage of Bloom's thoughts in the cemetery at Paddy Dignam's funeral in the sixth episode:

> Seat of the affections. Broken heart. A pump after all, pumping thousands of gallons of blood every day. One fine day it gets bunged up: and there you are. Lots of them lying around here: lungs, hearts, livers. Old rusty pumps: damn the thing else. The resurrection and the life. Once you are dead you are dead. That last day idea. Knocking them all up out of their graves. Come forth Lazarus! And he came fifth and lost the job. (*U*, 87)

Both represent a kind of internal dialogue of rhetorical question and answer, observation, speculation and aside.

Joyce clearly needs three full episodes for each character's story and reservoir of mental associations to be established and indeed to establish a kind of semantic norm of narration and inner monologue on which later departures can be based. But *Ulysses* proper – the *Ulysses* that does not so much extend the repertoire as exploit and explode the atomic structure of narrative – post-culturalist *Ulysses* – only gets fully underway in the seventh episode set in the offices of the

Dublin newspapers the *Freeman's Journal* and the *Evening Telegraph*.
There are a number of things about the episode that contribute to
the sense of its importance. Both dialectical and dialogical, it is the
first episode in which both Bloom and Stephen appear and in which
neither may be said to dominate the narrative point of view. Bloom in
this hour does the best part of his whole day's work, so economics get
full attention as do the nationalist political rhetorics of the day. As
Lawrence (1981) points out, the episode was revised late in the process of composing the novel in 1921 (the conspicuous headlines were
added at this late stage) and so it bears the marks of later experiment
on earlier material in a interesting way. Here too the implied narrator's
technique, previously eccentric but broadly reliable, takes on new
manic energies, describing the scene in a succession of verbal patterns
drawn from the repertoire of classical rhetoric.

The newspaper setting provides a social and a literary location in
which both Faustian intellectual Stephen and urban survivor Bloom
can credibly be present: a *New Grub Street* of the Irish literary revival.
More deeply still it opens up a whole range of questions about the discursive pressures under which and the discursive space in which both
can function or at least survive in the modern, post-industrialised,
urban world of mass communication and commerce. To that extent it
may be thought of as a portrayal of what Walter Benjamin (1973)
called 'The Work of Art in the Age of Mechanical Reproduction'.

The massive engines of printing that come to life in this chapter –
quite literally the means of literary production – are in the hands of the
florid, raucous burgers of Dublin whose extravagant verbality makes
up the substance of its dialogue. Stephen's dreadful drunken father
fares well in this environment and speaks its language. 'Agonising
Christ', he says about the florid poeticisms of a political speech that
has been reported in the paper and is quoted at length in the episode,
'wouldn't it give you a heartburn on your arse?'

Two editors, the ceremonial William Brayden of the *Freeman* (who
recannibalising Mulligan's 'stately' entry at the start of the book enters
this scene 'statelily', *U*, 3 and 97) and the brazen, loutish Myles Crawford of the *Telegraph*, dominate the world of print. Neither have much
time for the kind of poetry that Stephen has scribbled on the torn-off
corner of Deasy's letter and for whose meaning Stephen himself is
forced to drag his memories of Dante's *Inferno*. For Crawford the torn
page suggests no more than that someone was 'short taken'. The

sponger Lenehan's limerick about 'Professor' MacHugh or his dreadful joke about the rows of cast steel/*Rose of Castile* have more chance of getting into this paper. Bloom, though, has a viable corner to work: the interface between the press and the world of commerce. He digs out an old advertisement for the tea merchant Alexander Keyes that he can revamp with a new logo which subliminally suggests the 'Innuendo of home rule'. That one economical idea serves simultaneously to flatter the interests of Keyes, the newspaper, the dominating political ideology of the Home Rulers and thereby assists Bloom's own pocket and the economic support of his family. It even leaves enough left over for the late night offer of hospitality to Stephen that is to come. Advertising and the advertising image are already seen as the low but viable artistic products of this post-literate consumerist city world. Bloom is alert enough to such social change to be encouraging his daughter into a career in the new technology of photography.

But English language prose narrative may itself (as a glance at the Renaissance prose works of Deloney or Nashe confirm) be said to be another artistic product of burgher civilisation, and it is in the short narrative that Stephen himself offers on the way to Mooney's bar at the close of the episode that a further clue to the importance of the episode may reside.

MacCabe laboriously – even mistakenly – selects a number of moments in *Ulysses* (the reference to Bloom's 'other eye' in 'Sirens'; the '*Egomen*' in Stephen's thoughts in 'Scylla' and the parodic comment 'I have often thought since on looking back') as examples of the book referring to itself or to its reader. None is so interesting as the moment in 'Aeolus' when, in introducing his 'Parable of the Plums', Stephen thinks to himself the single word 'Dubliners'. Without necessarily disrupting the plausible sequence of Stephen's thoughts, this should strike any reader as a reference to Joyce's own volume of stories published under that title and as such represents an extraordinarily explicit kind of extra-textual self-cannibalisation of which Brayden's entry noted above is an intra-textual example.

Though by no means identical with the *Dubliners* stories, Stephen's story seems set up as a paradigm of the kind of spare and realistic denunciation of urban constraint that Joyce had offered as his first literary effort to the *Irish Homestead*. It is set up as a normative or chaste narrative against the promiscuous narrative trickery of the episode. An *ad hoc* extrapolation of the Bakhtinian terms 'monologic' and 'dialogic' may clearly help us to contrast this narrative norm from what, by time of the 'Aeolus' episode, *Ulysses* had become (Lodge, 1983).

The arguably simple story is dialogised first in the very literal sense by the fact that it is presented within and is interrupted by narrative and dialogue. But then it is subject to all the other carnivalisations of narrative that characterise the episode. It is superdialogised by the interior monologues of both Stephen and Bloom that occur during its telling. We might say that it is hyperdialogised by the arbitrary rhetorical tropes that decorate the narrative and, furthermore, that it is meta-metadialogised by the newspaper headlines that interrupt it commenting on the story itself, on the incidents that interrupt its telling and (meta-meta-metadialogically?) on the discussion of the story by its hearers. This discussion itself provides a meta-meta-dialogical level, proposing alternatives to the reader for reading the story either as a novelty or satire full of obscenity and private jokes (Myles Crawford, *U*, 121–3) or, following up the Moses rhetoric, as an inverted parable against Home Rule (Professor MacHugh, *U*, 122–3) or as a piece of austere realism (Crawford's question 'Where did they get the plums?', *U*, 122, is one that the story has already answered!). Bakhtin's emphasis on the burgherly ritual of carnival must surely help us too to place the brash processional of figures through this episode in context. By the end of this episode, in narrative terms, we have climbed a long way. 'SOME COLUMN!' as the headline (albeit falsely) says the Dublin vestals say.

THE PALIMPSEST OF IDENTITY

The dazzling and hilarious fragments of Stephen's psuedo-theory of Shakespeare represent the next stage of development in his quest to read 'the signatures of all things' and their manic or perverse brilliance provides us with a 'cracked looking glass' or prototype of the reading that we bring to *Ulysses* itself. The encounter with Shakespeare explodes the formalist and anti-authorial assumptions of Stephen's early Aristotelianism. Aristotle now offers him a 'possibility theory': a model of the mind as a myriad of conflicting possibilities of which only a few can become actualities in life but many more may be explored in art.

Technically the episode suggests still further dialogisation with one vital snatch of dialogue and action transmitted only through Stephen's inner monologue (*U*, 158, 9.301–3) another (within Stephen's inner monologue or not?) translated into Shakespearean Miltonic blank verse (*U*, 167, 9.683–706) and a third written in the parody of the written form of dramatic dialogue that is to be used throughout the 'Circe' episode (15) later in the book (*U*, 171–2, 9.893–934). If Stuart Gilbert described the passage of the soap in Bloom's pockets throughout the day as a 'saponiad', then this should presumably be called a 'dialogiad' running through the episode.

Stephen reads Shakespeare's plays as a multiple self-projection from certain traumatic incidents in his life. There is an undeniable flavour of Freudian psychology here but Freud's repressed Oedipal love of mother and son does not interest Stephen so much as the sexual traumas produced by Shakespeare's relationship with Anne Hathaway and the mystical/psychological puzzle of paternity. If there is a hidden incestuous anxiety to be explored, he finds it in the far more deeply repressed homosexual incestuous relationship of father and son who are:

> sundered by a bodily shame so steadfast that the criminal annals of the world, stained with all other incests and bestialities, hardly record its breach. Sons with mothers, sires with daughters, lesbic sisters, loves that dare not speak their name, nephews with grandmothers, jailbirds with keyholes, queens with prize bulls. (*U*, 170)

Dedalus – named from the builder of the labyrinth to entrap the offspring of one such bestial coupling – has already discovered in the Cork episode of *A Portrait* the paradoxical act of self-fathering performed by the writer's imagination. If incest is itself a kind of self-legitimation, this self-fathering is an ultra-incestuous act glimpsed in the image of the artist's endogamous or incestuous hoarding that Stephen conjures up in virtuoso response to Eglinton's dare that he 'Prove Shakespeare was a Jew'. The act of being a father to oneself is glimpsed too in the theological mysteries of the heretics: another analogy for the heretical act of the production of selves out of the self that is implied in the act of dramatic composition raucously reglossed in Mulligan's masturbatory pseudo-Freudian spoof of the theory written out in playbill form: 'Everyman His Own Wife or a Honeymoon in the Hand' (*U*, 178).

Another element of Stephen's interpretative method that may remind us of Freud is the belief that there is no such thing as insignificant error. 'A man of genius makes no mistakes', he says of Shakespeare's problematic marriage, 'His errors are volitional and are the portals of discovery' (*U*, 156). There may also be Freud in Stephen's interpretative use of polysemy as a way of undercutting assumed identities and establishing new and disturbing ones. 'What's in a name?' ask Stephen's interlocutors and with good reason. His theory points to the characters in Shakespeare's plays (Anne, Edmund, Gilbert, Richard) who share names with the members of the playwright's family, thereby implying that in creating them Shakespeare was consciously or unconsciously working out his own anxieties. Above and beyond that Stephen implies that identity itself may (in the great 'fiction' of the world) be predetermined by naming. Shakespeare's permissive name-punning in the sonnets and in John of Gaunt's death speech legitimate Stephen's associations and neither he (as Dedalus) nor his listeners are free from the tyranny of the name. 'That's my name Richard, don't you know', says Best. Here Freud looks forward to the predetermining linguistic structures built into the psychoanalytic theories of Jacques Lacan and to the interpretative dependence on polysemantic *brisure* in Jacques Derrida. The providential character of multi-lingual pun – *Hamlet* is *'pièce de Shakespeare'* but also Hamlet is a piece of Shakespeare – legitimises Stephen's theorising. And in his version, the self-punning astrologer-playwright Shakespeare reads his name and identity in the great W of the constellation Cassiopeia: quite literally, that is, in the stars.

Predeterminations and assumed identities in language are matched by a similar series of analogies between lives and narrative situations by which Stephen creates a map or key of cultural translation or revision, which beyond Freud's Oedipal key linking Greek myth and modern domestic life links Shakespeare's life – to the plot of Hamlet, to his other works, to the life of Christ. And beyond the character of Stephen, Joyce himself adds analogies to Stephen's life, the life of Bloom, the life of Odysseus, the lives of Aristotle and Socrates and, of

2 Shakespeare and company: the palimpsest of identity

	Fathers	Sons	Seduction by older woman
Life of Shakespeare	John Shakespeare, butcher, applied for coat of arms; d. 1601 on eve of writing *Hamlet*	Hamnet d. 1596 at age 11	Anne Hathaway 26, Shakespeare 18 on marriage in 1582; daughter Suzanne born five months later
Hamlet	Shakespeare played the ghost of old Hamlet; Polonius as father		
Other plays	Lear, Cymbeline, Pericles, Prospero, Henry IV	Death of Prince Arthur in *King John*	Venus in 'Venus and Adonis', Cressida in *Troilus and Cressida*; also 'shrews'
Bloom	Father's suicide	Rudy, d. 11 weeks, vision of him at 11	Molly (past), Bella Cohen, Bridie Kelly
Stephen	Drunken Simon Dedalus/mythic Daedalus		Prostitute in a *A Portrait*
Life of Joyce	Decline of John Joyce's fortune; 'Ecce Puer' poem	Giorgio and Lucia Joyce	Nora
The Odyssey	Odysseus	Telemachus; searching motif	Penelope abandoned
Life of Christ	God the Father/ Joseph	Jesus	
Others	Daedalus	Icarus	Socrates' Xanthippe; Aristotle's Phyllis

course, the life of Joyce himself.

Identity is a palimpsest. A table of implied identities can be drawn up based on father–son relationships and on interrelated complexes of sexual initiation by an older woman, the banished husband, sexual insecurity and/or promiscuity, the faithful/unfaithful wife, the

Cuckold/ exile	Wife, faithful/ unfaithful	'Other' women etc.	Brother/ adulterer	Grandchild
Time in London	Anne Hathaway, bequest to her of 'secondbest' bed	Mary Fitton, Penelope Rich, burgher's wife, Young man, Bankside punks	Edmund, Richard, Gilbert	Born to Elizabeth
Old Hamlet Hamlet Polonius?	Gertrude Ophelia		Claudius	
Othello, Prospero, Posthumus Leonatus Duke and Orlando in *As You Like It*	'hell of time' of tragedies, Dark Lady, Anne in Richard III, etc.	Cleopatra	Jachimo Richard III Edmund, Tarquin, Iago, Young man	Children of late plays
Bloom as cuckold	Molly (present)	Martha Clifford, Gerty MacDowell, Zoe	Boylan, Mulvey, etc.	Milly
Artistic exile	E—C—	Whores in nighttown and Paris	Cranly, Mulligan	
Artistic exile	J's fears of 1909	Amalia Popper, M. Fleischman, G. Kaempffer	Curran, Gogarty, Prezioso, Stanislaus	Stephen, Joyce?
Wanderings	Penelope as type of chastity	Calypso Circe, etc.	Suitors	Nostos homecoming
Joseph Christ's ministry	Mary Helen as type of unchastity	Mary Magdalene, Martha and Mary	Holy Ghost, Angel of Annunciation	Assumption

deceiving friend or brother, and the reconciliatory experience of grandchildren. It results in a unique and complex picture of the deep structure of patriarchal authority and hetero-homosexual family complexes, built into the texture of our central cultural artefacts: not so much an Oedipus as an Odysseus complex.

Reading and writing themselves (whether for Shakespeare, Stephen, Joyce or for anyone else) may be inseparable from the need to find or create one's place within this palimpsest of identity. So Bloom's thoughts on being handed an evangelising leaflet at the start of the previous episode (8) suggest:

> Bloo . . . . Me? No.
> Blood of the Lamb.   (*U*, 124)

So too does the product of his first juvenile literary ambitions, remembered in 'Ithaca' (17):

> An ambition to squint
> At my verses in print
> Makes me hope that for these you'll find room.
> If you so condescend
> Then please place at the end
> The name of yours truly, L. Bloom.   (*U*, 554)

Bloom, as the preceding passage informs us, was able at an early age to realise the folly of applying 'to the works of William Shakespeare more than once for the solution of difficult problems in imaginary or real life' (*U*, 554). But neither he nor Stephen are able to exempt themselves from the cultural processes that determine their identities for whose clues they search the record in their different but increasingly complementary ways. Each is, like Mallarmé's Hamlet quoted in the episode, condemned by intertextuality to 'reading the book of himself'.

Applying such a model of reading to the reading of *Ulysses* throws up a number of relevant points. If Shakespeare is not young but old Hamlet, then Joyce is not Stephen but Bloom. *Ulysses* thus further enacts the transfer of writerly authority from the Arnoldian poet/priest Stephen to the modern post-cultural writer/advertising man Bloom that we saw in 'Aeolus'.

Since for Joyce to write *Ulysses* was to rely on the famous Homeric compositional scaffold, to read the book can also be to embark on a vast cultural Odyssey searching for this and for others of the kinds of analogies that are keyed together in the Shakespeare theory. Not least we may wonder how the Homeric analogy itself works in this 'Scylla and Charybdis' episode. Most commentators see Stephen here as the figure whose precarious dialectical voyage through the episode, steering between dogma and mysticism, makes him the Odysseus of the moment – though Joyce's own note identifies Ulysses with Socrates, Jesus and Shakespeare. Bloom himself is not absent throughout. Indeed it is he who leaves the library 'between' the self-destructively brilliant Stephen and the mocking Mulligan at the end. And the final quotation in the episode – itself the closing speech from *Cymbeline* – sends us off to that subtext with questions of analogy and the interpretation through analogy that may follow.

Whether thought by Stephen or Bloom or neither one, the 'Druid' peacefulness of the quotation reminds us of the miraculous reconciliations at the end of Shakespeare's play that are confirmed by a soothsayer who explicates the prophetic punning mystery of the hero Posthumus Leonatus's name. Posthumus, married to the British Princess Imogen but banished and then duped like Othello into believing his wife unfaithful, fails to have her killed, is himself believed by her to be dead, helps ('posthumously'?) to defeat but then is imprisoned by the Romans, before being reunited with her at last. A feeble husband whose trust of his wife is vindicated and whose doubt is purged through extraordinary chaos, Leo-natus or lion-born, the lion's whelp of the prophecy may provide another palimpsestic prophecy of – or else a vision that is in ironic contrast with – some kind of ultimate domestic vindication for Leo-pold Bloom.

DIVERGING PERSPECTIVES

Between the midday of the newspaper office, where Bloom and Stephen are both present and the midnight of the brothel, where their paths join, the pace and character of stylistic variation escalates and becomes more extravagant. Bloom's experiences dominate during the afternoon but, after having taken a position so deeply internal to Bloom's consciousness over lunch in 'Lestrygonians', the narrative experiments with a variety of different points of view on Bloom just as the funeral episode had given us an alternative perspective (from Bloom and Simon Dedalus) on Stephen Dedalus as he walked by (*U*, 73).

In the mid-afternoon and at the mid-point of the tenth episode, 'Wandering Rocks', Joyce's 'cracked looking glass' (to borrow Stephen's definition of Irish art from earlier in the day) refracts the simultaneous and interlocking actions of a range of Dublin's city dwellers beginning with Father Conmee, whose 'cheerful decorum' puts him in a line of fictional priests from Chesterton to Graham Greene. Besides Stephen at an Italian lesson and later, like Bloom, at a Liffeyside bookcart, the cinematic portraits glimpse the undertaker (and evidently police informer) Corny Kelleher in his office; Stephen's motherless sisters in their squalor; a beggar passing Molly's window in Eccles Street; Boylan's secretary Miss Dunne; Boylan flirting with a shopgirl as he buys Molly a seducer's gift; the grain-merchant and amateur historian Ned Lambert; the bragging 'chief bottlewasher' Lenehan; tea salesman Tom Kernan with his secondhand coat; Simon Dedalus with Father Cowley and Ben Dollard; lawyer's clerk Martin Cunningham taking up a collection for Paddy Dignam's family; Mulligan and Haines discussing Stephen; the eccentric Farrell; young Patrick Dignam; and the Earl of Dudley, the Viceroy, in his carriage complete with brass band on the way to open a charity bazaar.

Nowhere in literature is the extraordinary edifice of urban community so particularised or the variety and hidden inter-dependence of city lives so accurately reflected. The impression of intricate simultaneity is reinforced by mysterious fragmentary interpolations that occur in each section. Never was literature more like a crossword puzzle, or puzzles so richly and importantly communicative. A precarious mutual beggary characterises the economics of the city but its clogged sexuality is also laid bare. Conmee Jesuitically ponders the upper-class adultery of Mary Rochford through the legitimising formula of sex '*inter vas naturale*', while a mysterious couple (identified some three hundred pages later as Lynch and his girl, *U*, 339, 14.1153–4) emerge from the bushes beside him (*U*, 184). Bloom reads his mild pornography and Miss Dunne her romances. Lenehan gives a leering account of his trip with Molly. Boylan flirts and plans his afternoon's seduction and Farrell's odd comment '*Coactus Volui*' calls up the paradoxical perversity of Wilde's homosexuality.

We may even be tempted to investigate some potential 'reader-traps' of the type identified by Stuart Gilbert (1930). Might Boylan's

Text continues on p. 85

3 Wandering Rocks: themes and interpolations

1.	Father Conmee	180–4
2.	Corny Kelleher and Constable 57C	184–5
3.	One-legged sailor begging in Eccles Street	185–6
4.	Katey and Boody Dedalus in the kitchen	186–7
5.	Boylan buys basket of fruit for Molly	187
6.	Stephen's Italian lesson at Trinity	188
7.	Boylan's secretary Miss Dunne	188–9
8.	Ned Lambert in St Mary's Abbey	189–90
9.	Lenehan with Rochford and McCoy	191–3
10.	Bloom at a bookshop	193–4
11.	Dilly Dedalus begs money from her father	195–6
12.	Tom Kernan preens himself	196–8
13.	Stephen at a bookcart	198–200
14.	Simon Dedalus meets Cowley and Dollard	200–2
15.	Martin Cunningham takes up a collection	202–4
16.	Mulligan and Haines at the Bakery	204–5
17.	The eccentric Fitzmaurice Tisdall Farrell	205–6
18.	Master Patrick Dignam	206–7
Coda	The Viceroy's cavalcade	207–9

The interpolations

Scattered irregularly through 15 of the 18 sections are 31 interpolations (definable as intrusions of simultaneous narrative action that are strictly invisible in terms of the narrative economy of that section). [Two other apparent interpolations (given by Blamires, 1988, and by Gifford and Seidman, 1988) – the glimpse of Father Conmee in Corny Kelleher's section 4 (*U*, 185) and the appearance of Councillor Nannetti on the steps of the City Hall in section 15 (*U*, 202) would only qualify if we said that the actions were visible to but not remarked by the characters present.] Of these (to try to employ Gilbert's formula for them strictly) only nine (in order of appearance nos. 2, 4, 5, 8, 10, 11, 19, 20 and 21) consist in excerpts from the action of other sections. A larger group of eleven (nos. 3, 7, 9, 13, 14, 15, 25, 26, 27, 29, 30) should more accurately be described as anticipations or continuations of the action of other sections, since they contain additional information to that which is contained in the respective sections themselves.

Another group of seven interpolations (Maginni in sections 1 and 10; Richie Goulding in section 9 and the 'elderly female' in sections 9 and 10; Dennis and Mrs Breen in section 12; the two women in section 13; the Ormond barmaids in section 15, nos. 1, 16, 12, 17, 23, 24 and 28) have no real home in the action of one or other of the eighteen sections but the simultaneity of their action is confirmed by the reappearance of the characters (at these or other moments during their activities) beside the viceregal cavalcade. The three appearances of the floating, screwed-up throwaway leaflet in sections 4, 12 and 16 (nos. 6, 22 and 31) need no such justifications. They are interpolations with no 'home section' in this episode though we may find one in the last-but-one 'Lestrygonians' episode. The remaining interpolation, the cycle race in section 11 (no. 18), has no 'home section' either, but is partly anticipated by Bloom (*U*, 5.551–3) and remembered by Gerty (*U*, 13.134–5) as I explain in the text.

Line numbers of interpolations by section

1. 1, ll. 56–60.
2. 2, ll. 222–3.
3. 3, ll. 236–7.
4. 4, ll. 264–5; 5, l. 281; 6, ll. 294–7.
5. 7, ll. 315–6.
6. None.
7. 8, ll. 373–4; 9, ll. 377–9.
8. 10, l. 425; 11. 441–2.
9. 12, ll. 470–5; 13, ll. 515–6; 14, ll. 534–5; 15, ll. 542–3.
10. 16, ll. 599–60; 17, ll. 625–631.
11. 18, ll. 651–3; 19, ll. 673–4; 20, ll. 709–10.
12. 21, ll. 740–1; 22, ll. 752–4; 23, ll. 778–80.
13. 24, ll. 818–20; 25, ll. 842–3.
14. 26, ll. 919–20; 27, ll. 928–931.
15. 28, ll. 962–3; 29, ll. 984–5.
16. 30, ll. 1063–4; 31, ll. 1096–9.
17. None.
18. None.
Coda None.
False interpolations 2, ll. 213–4 and 15, ll. 970–1.

Line numbers of short-titled interpolations by the section in which they appear. For excerpts the home section (hs) and for anticipations, continuations etc. the other section(s) in which the material appears (os) are given in parenthesis.

1. 1, Maginni, ll. 56–60 (os. 10, Coda).
2. 2, Molly, ll. 222–3 (hs. 3).
3. 3, O'Molloy, ll. 236–7 (os. 8).
4. 4, Conmee, ll. 264–5 (hs. 1); 5, The Lacquey's bell, l. 281 (hs. 11); 6, Throwaway, ll. 294–7 (os. 12, 16).
5. 7, Bloom, ll. 315–6 (os. 10).
6. None.
7. 8, Rochford's machine, ll. 373–4 (hs. 9); 9, Hely's men, ll. 377–9 (os. 9).
8. 10, Parnell's brother, l. 425 (hs. 16); 11, Lynch's girl, ll. 441–2 (hs. 1).
9. 12, Goulding/elderly female, ll. 470–5 (os. Coda); 13, Cavalcade, ll. 515–6 (os. Coda); 14, Master Dignam, ll. 534–5 (os. 16); 15, Molly, ll. 542–3 (os. 3).
10. 16, Maginni, ll. 599–60 (os. 1, Coda); 17, Elderly female, ll. 625–631 (os. 9, Coda).
11. 18, Cycle race, ll. 651–3 (none); 19, Kernan, ll. 673–4 (hs. 12); 20,

Cavalcade, ll. 709–10 (hs. Coda).
12. 21, Cowley and Dedalus, ll. 740–1 (hs. 14); 22, Throwaway, ll. 752–4
     (os. 4, 16); 23, Dennis and Mrs Breen, ll. 778–80 (os. Coda).
13. 24, Two women, ll. 818–20 (os. Coda); 25, Conmee, ll. 842–3
     (os. 1, 4).
14. 26, Farrell, ll. 919–20 (os. 17); 27, Hugh C. Love, ll. 928–931 (os. 8).
15. 28, Barmaids, ll. 962–3 (os. Coda); 29, Boylan, ll. 984–5 (os. 5, 6).
16. 30, One-legged sailor, ll. 1063–4 (os. 3); 31, Throwaway, ll. 1096–9
     (os. 4, 12).
17. None.
18. None.
Coda None.
False interpolations 2, ll. 213–4 and 15, ll. 970–1.

---

typist-secretary Miss Dunne (Bloom is said to phone 'unspeakable messages' to a 'Miss Dunn at an address in D'Olier street' in 'Circe' *U*, 438, 15.3029–30) be none other than the Martha Clifford who types Bloom naughty letters? Might Molly's 'onelegged sailor' be none other than the D. B. Murphy we are to meet later in the day? May he in turn be the sailor Mulvey of Molly's memory (Gordon)? The detailed cross-correspondences of the episode call for some kind of enumerative or explanatory chart.

Earlier in the day Bloom has seen an advert for a cycle race:

> He eyed the horseshoe poster over the gate of college park: cyclist doubled up like a cod in a pot. Damn bad ad. Now if they had made it round like a wheel. (*U*, 70, 5.551–3)

The cyclists themselves are glimpsed and named in one of the simultaneous interpolations as they 'negotiated the curve by the College library' (*U*, 195, 10.651–3). In 'Nausicaa' Gerty longs romantically for her Regie Wylie, evidently the brother of one of these men (*U*, 287, 13.135). The details interlock and recur but the styles in which they are treated differ radically according to the diverging stylistic trajectories taken by the later episodes of the book.

Some episodes may not depend so directly for their technical distinctiveness on a sense of perspective or point of view. In the 'Sirens' chapter, in which Bloom can be found along with Dedalus, Dollard, Cowley and Tom Kernan in the bar of The Ormond Hotel, the style is a kind of intoxication or infection of the narrative discourse by musical form, responsive more to interpersonal factors of mood and situation. A device like this seems to threaten and challenge readerly assumptions about narrative at a very deep level and inaugurates new kinds and levels of complexity.

The paradigm of stylistic variation that is relatable to perspective – especially distanced perspectives on Bloom – does, however, help us to digest the late-afternoon episodes. The intolerant nationalism of the unnamed narrator of the 'Cyclops' episode in Barney Kiernan's bar (itself retrospectively re-narrated from Bloom's point of view in 'Eumaeus', *U*, 16.1081–7) is followed by the romanticised perspective of Gerty MacDowell on the beach in 'Nausicaa': she on Bloom (*U*, 292–301, 13.365ff) and Bloom on her (*U*, 301, 13.772–9). Even here, though, stylistic variation can by no means entirely be explained by variations in perspective and point of view. The Cyclopean narrator's rantings in episode 12 are made yet more extraordinary by the interpolation of an increasingly absurd series of thirty-three parodies, recasting Bloom as a hero of medieval romance (no. 3), recalling scenes from Irish history, like the hanging of Robert Emmet (no. 7) and so on. Gerty herself is seen by some not so much as a character but as a parody of the sentimental romance fiction that she reads. The recapitulatory procession parodying English prose from its sub-Latinate origins to the latest American slang that makes up the 'Oxen of the Sun' episode (14) reinforces a sense of language operating by its own self-generating logics, beyond the control of the individual user, and prepares the reader for yet further developments.

The increasing size, scale and ambition of each successive episode, not to mention the enlarging gaps between episodes 12 and 13, 13 and 14, and 14 and 15, all contribute to a sense of wildly diverging and imaginative trajectories broadening and elaborately transgressing the apparent boundaries of the book.

THE GOD OF SIGNPOSTS

The climax or climaxes of the plot of *Ulysses* come in 'Circe', the fifteenth episode, set in Dublin's brothel district at midnight, which Joyce thought of as the 'last adventure' of Ulysses before his homecoming. Stylistically it may be thought the most extravagant episode and is undoubtedly the most dialogical, the most mixed, seeming to extend several of the lines of stylistic development proposed in earlier episodes (parody, unconscious thoughts, extreme perspectives) at one and the same time. Joyce's desire to create a new Ulyssean 'polytropism', as well as his ideas of drama increasingly conceived as a theatricalisation of prose narrative come to fruition here. Under the technical label 'hallucination', Joyce achieves a dream play of anarchic action mixed with ghostly and unconscious projection. Animated objects come to life and speak and a series of expanded stage directions themselves make up a surreal fantasy narrative.

Nietzschean theory of the origin of dramatic art in Dionysian ritual with its orgiastic frenzies, flagellations and transvestisms might well have helped Joyce to his conception of the episode as did his reading of Flaubert's semi-surreal *Temptation of St Anthony* and of the masochistic sexual fantasies of Sacher-Masoch and others. Carnival, both in its root sense of an ascetic 'farewell to the flesh' and in its modern sense of a burgherly processional festival or release, comes to mind, as do the frenzied counterpoints of musical fugue and the startling alternation of peaks and troughs in manic-depressive illness. But the clearest impression is one of the book wildly retranslating the material of the earlier episodes (Bloom's visit to the Butcher's, his meeting with Mrs Breen), of a book cannibalising and exploding itself.

The frenzied chaos and excitement of Joyce's composition of the episode, written just after he returned to Paris – the destinction of his first escape – in the summer and autumn of 1920, comes across in his letters. They record superstitious anxieties about typists and providential accumulations of material. He discovers modern equivalents for the moly plant that preserves Homer's hero (Bloom's potato) and for Hermes, the god who assists him. Hermes becomes 'the god of signposts' and, most Circeanly of all, is defined as 'the point at which roads parallel merge and roads contrary also' (*SL*, 272).

Joyce's brother wrote: 'I suppose "Circe" will stand as the most horrible thing in literature. I wish you would write verse again' (*L*, III, 58).

Structurally the episode is by no means easy to follow, since, like the wildest fantasy or dream, it strives to disrupt rather than to establish both realistic ground and causal sequence. The reader may barely hold on to the roller coaster of real and imaginary events.

First Stephen and Lynch and then Bloom make their entrances. Bloom is greeted by the ghosts of his parents and then by a vision of the Mrs Breen whom he has met earlier in the day and who now teases him more openly. He is questioned by the two soldiers of the watch and this turns into a trial of him as a sex criminal. When that illusion fades the English whore Zoe greets him and begins to tease him into Bella Cohen's where Stephen and Lynch have already gone. Before he enters, he undergoes a long hallucination in which he is variously transformed into a civic leader, exposed as a fake and then elevated again into a kind of messiah.

Finally inside the brothel the girls and their clients play at the end of the world and (with the help of the ghost of Bloom's grandfather) at being expert sexologists. Bella Cohen enters and immediately entraps Bloom in a masochistic scenario during which he is turned both into a woman and a pig, a domination from which he is only saved by his indulgence in and exposure of the subsidiary masturbatory fantasy of the nymph (who comes to life from the picture above the Blooms' bed).

Disillusion breeds financial wrangle but the party gets underway again and Stephen leads a dance to the tune of 'My Girl's A Yorkshire Girl' that becomes more and more frenzied until it calls up the ghost of his mother, which he can only banish by striking out the brothel gas-lamp with his ashplant stick and fleeing outside, leaving the more worldly Bloom to pay. Once outside Stephen gets into a fight with two foul-mouthed English soldiers who think he has insulted their girl and who knock him down to accompanying images of British Empire, the executed Irish rebel Croppy Boy and a Black Mass. Bloom and the sober undertaker Corny Kelleher are left to clear up and as Bloom cares for the paralytic prostrate figure of Stephen, an image of his dead son Rudy, as he would have been at eleven years old, comes into his mind.

Two contrasting moments among the many climaxes of this 'action' may help us to approach 'Circe'. The first is Bloom's liminal fantasy experienced in conversation with Zoe at the door of Bella Cohen's, a fantasy that is especially interesting since the genetic evidence suggests that it was first drafted independently of the evolving sequence of the whole (Herring, 1977). In the draft Bloom's fantasy of political leadership, disgrace and messianic victimisation begins with a parody of the viceregal cavalcade and ends with the litany of recapitulation – prime emblem of the literary impulse of the episode. Bloom's political programme promises to represent everybody in general but ends up offending everybody in particular. It might make sense to think of it as a kind of catholic emancipation, so 'catholic' and so 'emancipatory' that even (or perhaps especially) the Jesuit Father Farley protests with some reason that Bloom is 'an anythingarian, seeking to overthrow our holy faith' (*U*, 400). The prudish Mrs Riordan confirms that he is a 'bad man'.

Bloom's 'anythingarianism' contrasts with Stephen's cry of '*Nothung!*', made on exorcising the menacing spectre of his mother's ghost (*U*, 475), both terms having been added at a later stage in the drafting of the episode and providing a kind of labelling of it. In one sense Stephen's cry of 'Nothing' (as it read in the first draft) is a typical gesture of Faustian/Satanic denial. He may, like the Bob Dylan of the sleeve notes of *Bringing It All Back Home* (1965) be declaring 'i accept chaos. i'm not sure if chaos accepts me.' In another sense, by naming Siegried's sword 'Needful', it ties up the Wagnerian subtext which serves to hypostatise Stephen's youthful condition as one of self-destructive desiring, the '*Hangende Hunger*', which in Stephen's garbled quotation is said to '*Macht uns alle kaputt*' (*U*, 457). MacCabe goes further and in the bilingual polysemy of the cry finds Stephen's political desire to separate his fate from that of the Croppy Boy: to be 'not hung'. Beyond the merely nationalist context, it reveals Stephen's psycholinguistic liminality: a condition that is forever on the borders of those other worlds (whether the ineffable world of the spirit or the unspeakable world of the body) for which there is or seems to be 'no tongue'.

One of the most suggestive recent readings of the episode, by Daniel Ferrer, depends upon the psychoanalytical theories of Melanie Klein. Stephen's bereavement, according to Ferrer, requires that he regressively relive all the previous unconscious 'losses' of the mother, and the surrogate objects unconsciously created to replace her, from which the psychological experiences of desire and lack are derived. The regressive/recapitulatory structure and style of the episode as well as Stephen's own morbidly hyperactive imagination might seem to be explicable in this way. Were we to look, as Stephen does in the case of Shakespeare, for the significant coincidence of names between characters in *Ulysses* and in Joyce's own life, we could not help noticing that both his and Stephen's mothers were called May.

The death of the mother for both Stephen and Joyce might have been further complicated and indeed more deeply universalised by the self-willed but problematic separation from 'mother' Church, 'mother' Ireland and from the dying mother of language itself as a medium for narrative representation in the post-mechanised cinemato-photographic age, according to B. S. Johnson's *See the Old Lady Decently* (1975) at least.

For other readers Bloom's transformation scene is the definitive moment in the episode. Sandra Gilbert finds it an inadequate contribution to the sexual politics of androgyny, since Bloom is neither content to remain under Bella's domination nor to retain his cross-gendered identity. Sexual-political readings of the fantasy may have some validity since Joyce's reading of masochistic pornography may well have highlighted the socio-political aspects of sexual domination for him (Brown, 1985). Gilbert's sense of Bloom's failure, however, is not only humourless and overliteral but seems quite wrong since both he and Stephen clearly need to problematise their own positions as men within repressive spiritual and psychosexual structures of matriarchal authority during this episode and the book as a whole.

Joyce's early gloss of the episode to Frank Budgen seems much more sensible and down to earth. Here he said (suggesting the farcical moment when Bloom's button bursts) that moly might be 'laughter, the enchantment killer' and he refers to the 'knock out blow' of the end which 'brings all things back to their sordid reality' (*L*, I, 144). That sordid reality is, of course, money, the discussion of which haunts the episode from Bella's Guinness Preference Shares to Bloom's protection of Stephen's assets.

As well as being a location for dramatic riot, a symbol of sexual excess and of imperial victimisation, the brothel is a primary symbol for consumerist society at its logical extension: everything is done for money; everything is for sale. Here Stephen, the intellectual, is victim to political violence and needs protection from himself and from others, and here Bloom, the interstitial citizen, is at his most vulnerable and abused. Here too, where fetishism is a commodity, commodities have become fetishised, both in the modern social sense of Marxian economic theory and in the sense that objects (Bella's fan, Lynch's cap, the Nymph and so on) come to life. If, as Franco Moretti says, the particular historical crisis to which *Ulysses* relates is the crisis of contemporary capitalist overproduction, the superfetation of images in the hallucination finds another explanatory context in a critique of the economic basis of society. Here the workshop of the artist has fallen into the hands of the Sorcerer's Apprentice whose story forms part of the literary subtext of Marx's *Manifesto*.

Of all the climaxes in the episode, the final one, Bloom's vision of Rudy, seems the quietest, the most recessive, and the least easy to use as an interpretative focus of the whole. This is not the first time that *Ulysses* has played such a trick on us. Stephen's silent feelings of exclusion from Mulligan, his difficulty in coming to terms with the idea of love and Bloom's feeble defence of human morality to the Citizen all represent similar soft centres of the book.

Part of the post-modern self-referentiality of this book we have already seen to consist in the way its leading characters are all in some way readers, each of whom may be said to offer alternative surrogacies for the heroic task of the reader him or herself. No doubt it adds great depth to the poignancy of the dream vision of Rudy that he too is seen in his only appearance in the text as piously studying a book. Even gentile readers of *Ulysses*, soon discovering the need for retrospective rereadings of the text in order to reconstruct materials refracted through the memorial arrangements of its characters, will find something to identify with in Bloom's image of his son reading 'from right to left'. As we read backwards through the text we note the recapitulation in this image of Bloom's earlier image of his father 'with his hagadah book, reading backwards' (*U*, 101) and may see ourselves in this and in the diurnal feat of the typesetter in 'Aeolus' who 'Reads it backwards first' (*U*, 101) (Senn, 1982).

THE MAN KILLER

The dialectic of *Ulysses* which contrasts the experiences of the two male protagonists has more than one synthesis at the end of the book. After the climax of their meeting in 'Circe', Joyce provides us with a further closure in the exhaustion of their wanderings and of the narrative style of 'Eumaeus'. *Ulysses* is a series of information systems, through which the reader voyages in search of some further (though decreasingly conclusive) knowledge or truth. 'Ithaca', which Joyce wrote was 'in reality the end', provides an extraordinary archive of detailed information of the kind that Beckett in *Murphy* called 'demented particulars'. Its questions and answers seem to tell us everything that we can know according to the preset disciplines of our cognitive discourses, without apparently being able to tell us what it might be that we really want to know, according to our unconscious desires.

The final episode provides yet another form of closure, whether resisting all closure (MacCabe, 1978), or else (Lawrence, 1981; Boyle in Hart and Hayman, 1974) providing a musical 'Coda' which sweeps up narrative details like the Viceroy's cavalcade at the end of 'Wandering Rocks'. The eight unpunctuated sentences of Molly's inner monologue return us to the relative narrowness of a narrative style that is defined by a single character's point of view. The work of her memory is what Benjamin called 'the Penelope work of recollection', pausing to ask whether such involuntary Proustian memory is not 'much closer to forgetting than what is usually called memory?' (Benjamin, 1973, p. 204).

Molly's mode of ultimacy, then, is that of fallible human memory, mixing, in Eliot's phrase, 'memory and desire', both human and also, as in Joyce's resonant description of her to Harriet Shaw Weaver, 'posthuman' (*SL*, 289) in some way. Her sensibility – even more resolutely somatic than Bloom's – Joyce explained in terms of four key words – 'because', 'bottom', 'woman' and 'yes' – that irregularly punctuate her monologue and subliminally suggest a bodily subtext of 'breasts', 'arse', 'womb' and 'cunt' (*SL*, 285) – adding to areas in which Molly's vocabulary is already quite rich.

Bloom's late return home sets off a chain of memories of the early days of their marriage and of her view of Bloom's relationships with other women. This soon becomes mixed with recent memories of her afternoon's ecstasies with Boylan and the beginnings of their affair, prompting a number of comparisons between the relationships. Such thoughts give way (by sentences 4 and 5) to deeper memories of sexual awakening with her first boyfriends, especially Mulvey, in Gibraltar as a girl. Then, by way of memories of her meeting with Bloom on her arrival in Dublin in 1887 and her well-developed fantasies about seducing Stephen, we return to the memory of her kiss with Bloom on Howth Head sixteen years ago.

By no means all of her thoughts are about sex. She offers many shrewd judgements on burgher Dublin, on 'sponger' Lenehan, and 'forlornlooking spectacle' Breen, on her maid, on a shopgirl who has insulted her and on a tradesman who has tried to cheat her. She understands Bloom's occupations and her own economic dependence on them but also enjoys and works at the singing that is her principal mode of daytime employment. She is also another of the book's readers, constructing a 'female canon' (unremarked in Scott's discussion of female canons, 1986) from the sensation novels of the 1860s lent her by her female friend Hester Stanhope (*U*, 622).

But whereas others are unable to read without seeing their own names (and she fantasises that her favourite author Paul de Kock got his 'nickname going about with his tube from one woman to another', *U*, 970), she positively dislikes books, such as *Moll Flanders* or *Molly Bawn*, that include her name. In this way and others she seems saner than those around her. Indeed examples can be found of each of the qualities Joyce listed as charactersitic of her 'perfectly sane full amoral fertilisable untrustworthy engaging shrewd limited prudent indifferent *Weib*' (*SL*, 285). In more ways than one the list of her qualities has a disruptively anti-stereotypical feel.

According to Joyce 'Penelope' was also 'more obscene than any preceding episode', though presumably not in the conventional sense that Stephen thinks of father – son incest as unthinkably obscene or that Bloom confesses his 'most revolting piece of obscenity' in 'Circe'. Bloom's morning defecation is included but a tactful exclusion may explain the fact that Joyce 'put the light out . . . when it came to the chamber performance' just as Molly did whilst teasing the 'fellow opposite' by her window (*U*, 921).

It may rather be in the radical alterity of her female-centred perspective, in the precise sense that her thoughts consist in material that is in some way invisible, repressed or excluded, that Molly is 'obscene'. In Molly Joyce discovers the significant repressed other in the conundrum of the book's real and implied consciousnesses up to that point, and retells and restructures those consciousnesses from that other's point of view. Indeed, to some extent Molly is the significant repressed other of all Joyce's works up to this point and, it might be argued, of much in respectable Victorian society and discourse that denied a voice to sexual passion especially from a female point of view.

On close examination Molly's monologue reveals a far-reaching survey of the kind of female sexual experience and female sexual fantasy that is only now, through the researches of Nancy Friday and others, becoming known. Although surviving unscathed, Molly has to run a gauntlet of flashers ('that disgusting Cameron highlander behind the meat market', *U*, 620, 18.544–50), gropers ('a lot of that touching must go in theatres', *U*, 631, 18.1042), and clothes fetishists (Bloom's leery father, *U*, 634 and 18.1064). While being able to tolerate many of the harmless fetishistic oddities of Bloom's sexual needs, she draws the line at activities like sado-masochism that leave her cold ('sure there's nothing for a woman in all that', *U*, 619, 18. 493–9). Many of her own fantasies are reciprocal with those of Bloom: his 'smutty photo' of a nun (*U*, 608, 18.22) with her fantasy of sex with a priest (*U*, 610, 18.119–121); her 'wish some man or other would take me sometime when hes there' (*U*, 610, 18.104-5) pre-enacted in fantasy in 'Circe' (*U*, 460–2, 16.3738–93); her pygmalionist fellatio (*U*, 638, 18.1352–2) with his fascination with the goddesses earlier in the day; the sight of coupling flies that sets off his memories of Howth and the sight of coupling dogs that led her to conceive Rudy; his voyeurism, her exhibitionism; his anal kiss, her fantasy of an extravagant coprophiliac attack on Dr Collins (*U*, 634, 18.1162). Henke (1990) suggests there may have been a Lesbian element in her relationship with Hester Stanhope (*U*, 622, 18.642–5) or indeed with Josie Breen (*U*, 612, 18.203–4), at least as significant as the homosexual elements implicit in the relationships of Stephen and Bloom. If Joyce's social Freudianism portrays society as repressed, then he undoubtedly offers one form of liberation in Molly Bloom. And if, since Foucault, we can no longer believe that all knowledge is 'liberating' and that sex knowledge may itself only be a continuation of the attempt to control sex for potentially authoritarian ends, we can at least see Molly's punning evasion of Father Corrigan's inquisition ('he touched me father . . . where and I said on the canal bank like a fool', *U*, 610, 18.107–8) as comic relief from that authority.

From the perspective of her gender men are 'others' This is evident in her much-discussed use of pronouns, in which it can be hard for a reader to make the necessary transitions or even, at times, to distinguish between the individuals to whom she refers (for example *U*, 637). Her perspective on her marriage to Bloom provides what is among the most rewarding and most interesting of the comparisons thrown up by the perspectival structure of the book. Their kiss on Howth Head, which Parrinder calls the 'ultimate symbol' of the book, is also the ultimate symbol of the bivocality of gender, since it is remembered by Bloom as a moment of mutual passionate abandon ('Hot I tongued her. She kissed me. I was kissed', *U*, 144) and recalled by her as 'the day I got him to propose to me' (*U*, 642–3). Carefully conceived alterity serves to make each, in more ways than one, a 'fellow opposite' to the other.

At times Molly can be extreme in her anti-masculism. She condones, for instance, the notorious man killer Mrs Maybrick on the grounds that 'she must have been madly in love', that 'some men can be dreadfully aggravating' and yet that 'theyre not brutes enough to go and hang a woman surely are they' (*U*, 613). On the other hand, considering a male 'hardened criminal', she judges that 'they ought to be all shot or the cat of nine tails' or else, for attacking an old woman, she says 'Id cut them off him so I would' (*U*, 630). At one point she declares that men in general 'ought to get slow poison the half of them' (*U*, 635).

She can be just as hard on women. By the switch of a circuit in Joyce's imaginative chronolgy, Mrs Riordan, the prudish 'Dante' of Stephen's childhood in *A Portrait*, reappears as having lived with the Blooms in the City Hotel in the 1893–4 of both books' pasts. She is still prudish, 'down on bathingsuits and lownecks', and bequeaths her money to the church, but her denial of sex is incomprehensible to Molly who remembers having been sexually arousing to and perhaps even sexually aroused by her dog (*U*, 608 and 626, 18.15 and 812–3).

Critics have always been divided about Molly. Some early critics found her culpably promiscuous and indiscriminating; others a powerful earth goddess of the body. Among more recent critics, Richard Ellmann (1972) rebukes both William Empson and Edmund Wilson for seeking a fixed concluson in the book's next day: Empson in an affair between Molly and Stephen; Wilson in a resumed domestic mastery on the part of Bloom. Ellmann argues for a detemporalised transcendent reading of Molly as a sacramental hymn to the human body and to human, marital, sexual love. Kenner (1980) responds with a reminder of Molly's logic of inconsistency and contradiction and of the sheer bulk of necessary information her monologue contains which keeps it on the level of the everyday.

Many such debates took place between early male readers of the book. But the final episode of *Ulysses* envisions modern female readers that may now be much easier to conceive for us, living as we do, in a time after the life and death of Marilyn Monroe. Sixties feminists debated whether her portrait debases and/or elevates women according to damaging stereotypical patterns, whether or not she is bed and body bound. It may not be sufficient to alleviate the anxiety (expressed in a different context by Angela Carter) that the term '*Fleisch*' in German can mean either 'flesh' or 'meat', but we can note that in Joyce's formulation '*Ich bin der Fleish der stets bejaht*' (I am the flesh that affirms) he substitutes the offending '*das*' with the more abstract article '*der*'. At any rate, post-Cixousian criticism opens up new territories for the discussion of the problematics of her monologue as a model for a new '*écriture feminine*' in which the bounds of male discourse can be broken, and the things for which even Stephen has 'no tongue' be expressed. The most brilliant of contemporary women critics may now take off from this platform.

For writers of the 1930s like Henry Miller and Anaïs Nin the writing of this episode was Joyce's greatest achievement, its flow the agency for the regeneration of a corrupt civilisaton and many of the techniques, if not the mood, of Beckett's middle and late prose can be traced to Molly Bloom. Of all of Joyce's published work it is in this section that his 1909 letters to Nora, so fiercely repressed in the literary consciousnesses of Gabriel Conroy and Stephen Dedalus, can be most clearly glimpsed in all their Keatsian reality. And they locate Molly as the final symbolic or surrogate reader in the book:

> and his mad crazy letters My Precious one everything connected with your glorious Body everything underlined that comes from it is a thing of beauty and of joy for ever something he got out of some nonsensical book that he had me always at myself 4 and 5 times a day sometimes and I said I hadnt   (*U*, 634)

Beyond Hélène Cixous's ideas of writing with the body (1976), Molly's reaction to the letters seems to imply a reading with the body that extends Ulyssean somaticism into an as-yet untheorised territory definable as an ultimate dialogism of gender.

READING LIST

Walter Benjamin, *Illuminations* (London: Fontana, 1973).
Harry Blamires, *The New Bloomsday Book* (London: Routledge,1988).
Hélène Cixous, 'The Laugh of the Medusa', trans. Keith and Paula Cohen, *Signs*, 1 (1976) pp. 875–93.
Seamus Deane, *Celtic Revivals* (London: Faber, 1982).

Richard Ellmann, *Ulysses on the Liffey* (London: Faber, 1972).

Richard Ellmann, *The Consciousness of Joyce* (London: Faber, 1978).

William Empson, 'Magnificent Cuckolds', *London Review of Books*, 24 January 1991, p. 12.

Daniel Ferrer, 'Circe, Regret and Regression', in *Post-Structuralist Joyce*, ed. Derek Attridge and Daniel Ferrer (Cambridge: Cambridge University Press, 1984).

Don Gifford and R. J. Seidman, *'Ulysses' Annotated* (Berkeley: University of California Press, 1988).

Sandra Gilbert, *No Man's Land* (New Haven: Yale University Press, 1988).

Stuart Gilbert, *Ulysses: A Study* (London: Faber, 1930; rev. edn 1952).

John Gordon, *James Joyce's Metamorphoses* (Dublin: Gill and Macmillan, 1981).

Michael Groden, *Ulysses in Progress* (Princeton: Princeton University Press, 1980).

Barbara Hardy, *Tellers and Listeners* (London: Athlone, 1975).

Clive Hart and David Hayman (eds), *Ulysses: Critical Essays* (California: University of California Press, 1974).

David Hayman, *Ulysses: The Mechanics of Meaning* (Madison: University of Wisconsin Press, 1970 rev. 1982).

Phillip Herring, *Joyce's Notes and Early Drafts for Ulysses* (Charlottesville: University Press of Virginia, 1977).

Jeri Johnson, '"Beyond the Veil": Ulysses, Feminism and the Figure of Women', *European Joyce Studies*, 1, ed. Christine van Boheemen (Amsterdam: Rodopi).

Hugh Kenner, *Ulysses* (London: Unwin, 1980).

Karen Lawrence, *The Odyssey of Style in Joyce's 'Ulysses'* (Princeton: Princeton University Press, 1981).

A. Walton Litz, 'The Genre of Ulysses', in The Theory of the Novel, ed. John Halperin (New York: Oxford University Press, 1974).

David Lodge, 'Double Discourses: Joyce and Bakhtin', *James Joyce Broadsheet*, 4 (June 1983) pp. 1–2.

Vicky Mahaffey, *Re-Authorising Joyce* (Cambridge: Cambridge University Press, 1986).

Franco Moretti, *Signs Taken for Wonders* (London: Verso, 1988).

William H. Quillian, 'Joyce's 1912 *Hamlet* Lectures', *James Joyce Quarterly* (Summer 1978) pp.18–63.

Fritz Senn, 'Righting *Ulysses*', in MacCabe (1982).

4

Finnegans Wake

THE BOOK OF THE NIGHT

According to the witnesses assembled by Richard Ellmann, Joyce, having completed his book of a single day, moved on to tackle a book of the night. Most agree that the *Wake*, with the darkness and ambiguity of its language, its shifting and merging scenes and identities, and its deep structure of repeated family relationships can properly be called a 'dream'. Critics such as Bekker (1982) and Norris (1974) show the relevance of the mechanisms of Freudian dream work. It may, as Edmund Wilson implied in his article 'The Dream of H. C. Earwicker', be possible to identify the dreamer, or even as subsequent critics such as Nathan Halper (in Dalton and Hart, 1966) and John Gordon (1986) have argued, to assign a place and date to the dream (19 March 1922 and 21 March 1938 respectively).

Yet the dream question is vexed. A talking ass (recalling Shakespeare's Bottom, Apuleius and the Balaam of the Book of Numbers) narrates the appearance of Shaun as a postman in III.i and his questioning in a way that resembles the narrative convention of medieval dream vision ('in a dream . . . methought . . . was heard', *FW*, 404.3–4) and he continues, though in slightly different mood, to tell of Jaunty Jaun's sermon to the girls in III.ii. But the narrative status of his dream is promptly undercut by the opening of III.iii where Shaun, now Yawn, is himself 'oscasleep asleep' and the previous events are described as his 'dream monologue' (*FW*, 474.04) and then further destabilised by the appearance of the sleeping Porter family, on what Hart (1962) takes as the basic realistic level of the book, who themselves both dream and wake in III.iv. These dreams may be different from that of the dead or dreaming figure of Finnegan in I.i or the HCE dreamer of I.iv, who remembers his sins as he dozes, or they may all be part of some larger dream whose dreamer may be Porter, Earwicker, the author, the 'ideal insomniac' reader, or some other named or unnamed party. Or, perhaps, as Norris (in Attridge, 1990) has argued, this loss of identity is precisely what dreams are all about.

The punning title of the *Wake* suggests that in this dream we may be experiencing in anticipation something of Hamlet's 'sleep of death', a reading reinforced by that of John Bishop (1986). As in more recent, if less ambitious fictional experiments, like William Golding's *Pincher Martin* (1956) or Flann O'Brien's *The Third Policeman* (1967), we may be entering the streams of consciousness of characters who are already dead. Developing the Gothic strains in the earlier works, the *Wake* puns and plays with Gothic and other myths and ideas of death and resurrection from the scholarly construction of literary immortality to 'Dracula's nightout' (*FW*, 145.32) and to the ancient Egyptians' handbook for immortality, *The Book of the Dead*.

Most readers (Campbell and Robinson, Tindall, Gordon, Rose and O'Hanlon and so on) construct from the shifting sands of meaning a 'plot summary': some kind of sub- or super-narrative, featuring as its central characters either the initial letter family of Earwicker and Plurabelle in book I, chapters ii–viii, the more conventionally domestic Porter family of book III, chapter iv, or else perhaps the popular song/mythical Tim Finnegan/Finn MacCool of book I, chapter i.

The *Wake* may not be a conventional narrative but we may have no alternative means of reading it other than by recourse to the rules and conventions provided by our experience of prose narrative, whether these conventions be understood to apply directly or else by contrast or inversion as in an anti-novelistic scheme. Place and scene may be as circumscribed as John Gordon's reconstruction of the Porter family house (Gordon, 1986), or as far reaching 'antitopically' as the 3000 named locations in Ireland and elsewhere mentioned by Louis Mink in his Gazeteer (1978). Characters may be as few as the nuclear Earwicker family of father and mother, two sons, daughter and family servants (listed, with variations, in the questions and answers of I.vi, as the *dramatis personae* of the dream-play of II.i, as symbols (*FW*, 299.F4), and as the sleeping Porters that introduce III.iv). Or they may extend to any or all of the six or seven thousand persons named by Adaline Glasheen in her *Third Census* (1977).

Character, in the sense of fictional representation of person, is so radically deconceptualised and so mixed in with the substance of language that few characters bear the same name twice without some potentially significant modification of its form. Characters may be identified with each other according to a bewildering scheme of potential analogies of name, form or function. The 'normative' (*FW*, 32.18) initial letters HCE and ALP spell out larger depersonalised forms, and for the separate or merged identities of such depersonalised familial forms Joyce used a semi-geometric system of signs or ideograms in his notes and letters that, thanks to McHugh (1976), have come to be known as 'sigla' (*FW*, 32.14, 119.19 and 229F4). Greek pantheistic or Hindu conceptions of the multiple personalities or 'avatars' of deities like Zeus or Vishnu and the concept of schizophrenia from Western psychopathology are among the analogies explored by Joyce for his fictional experiment with naming and identity.

If the deliberately anomalous Dublin-Jewish-cuckold-ad-man character of Bloom in *Ulysses* offered Joyce the possibility of exponential extrapolation, what can we say of the stuttering, guilt-ridden, Bristolian-viceroy-Viking, Protestant landlord, insect and mountain H. C. Earwicker, whose role as 'turnpiker' (and therefore gatekeeper) establishes a vital structural link between him and Shakespeare's equivocating drunken Porter in *Macbeth*, except that he is by sheer amalgamation as much as by ordinary representativeness the 'Here Comes Everybody' named in I.ii (*FW*, 32.18–19)? In some ways he might be thought of as the logical product of Stephen's 'possibility theory' of Shakespearean character projection in *Ulysses*. Among the notions offered by Joycean critics, Adaline Glasheen's idea of a 'dream theatre' and Atherton's of metempsychosis both continue to be suggestive but are limited. Post-modern notions of the breakdown of Enlightenment rationalism and of the economic individualism on which the rise of the novel form is based (Norris, 1974) and Post-Freudian and Lacanian notions of the emptiness of subjectivity within the processes of somatic and significatory systems (Snead, 1988) inform much modern criticism.

The *Wake*'s plot, as the mention of 'equivocation' and the law of polysemy both confirm, is a catholic (though not exclusively a Roman

Catholic) one. Narrative threads and situations may be as numerous and as various as the 1001 of Scheherezade's Arabian Nights but they are all tales told 'of the same' (*FW*, 5.29), that is, of HCE, his supposed crime or crimes, the battling of his two sons and daughter, Shem, Shaun and Issy, and his long-suffering wife ALP and her letter of vindication. In 'kirkeyaard' (*FW*, 201.31) language it is a family plot, whose family relationships are presented with a pan-Freudian understanding of buried incestuous conflicts and with a post-Wittgensteinian understanding of the role of language in establishing identities and resemblances as well as a post-Einsteinian understanding of relativity.

Brief but impactedly surreal narrative interludes and set pieces greet the reader at every turn. Each may provide a place of entry for the concentrated study of the work: the tour of the 'museyroom', the Mutt and Jute dialogue and the much-analysed story of Jarl van Hoother and the Prankquean in I.i; Shaun's self-justificatory fables of 'Mookse and Gripes' in I.vi and 'Ondt and Gracehoper' in III.i (the latter glossed by Joyce himself in a letter to Harriet Weaver of 26 March 38, *SL*, 329–32); the encounter of HCE and the Cad in I.ii; the show trials of Festy King in I.iv, and of Yawn in III.iii, at the end of which Earwicker, through the mediation of his saintlier son, makes a long-awaited defence of himself; the parody of the *Book of Kells* in I.v; the self-incarceration of Shem in I.vii and the gossiping of the washerwomen in I.viii; the stories of the marriage of the tailor's 'dopter' to the errant Norwegian Captain and of the hesitant Buckley's shooting of the Russian General in II.iii; the old men's story of Tristan's seduction of Isolde in II.iv; the haunting last speech of Mrs Porter ('It is for me goolden wending', *FW*, 619.24) or her daughter ('Taks to you, taddy', *FW*, 619.33–4) in book IV.

These sections – often composed as separate episodes or sketches – are intricately embedded in a larger structural scheme whose sequential logic can defeat even devoted readers of the book. Joyce's structural sense of the punning interrelatedness of each with all permitted him to accept as providential what a more conventional author might have rejected as irrelevant. When Harriet Weaver commissioned a piece on the 'Giant's Grave' in St Andrew's churchyard in Penrith (*SL*, 316–18), he not only obliged but placed the passage on the opening page of the book. In the *Wake*, inverting the usual novelistic sense that digressions are puzzling and ambiguous diversions from the main thread, the polydigressive rule of structure can make the 'digressions' stand out as the clearest parts of the whole.

In the simplest outline this sequential whole consists of four books, comprising seventeen chapters. The first book is made up of eight chapters (I.i–viii), the first being a kind of overture to the whole in which Tim Finnegan, apparently killed partly as a result of the Wall Street Crash, wakes up at his wake. The next three recount the name and supposed crimes of HCE, his trial and self-incarceration. The fifth discusses the lost or partially destroyed letter that will, hopefully, vindicate him, while the sixth consists of twelve questions and answers posed and answered by and about Finn MacCool/HCE and his family. The seventh tells the story of his corpo- and coprographic forger/writer son Shem and the eighth is a dialogue between two washerwomen about his wife ALP.

There are four chapters in the second book (II.i–iv). In the first of them, the reprobate Glugg (another Shem) is teased by his sister Izod and a group of twenty-eight monthly-rainbow-girl 'Floras' in a sexual-riddling evening children's game, in which he has to guess the colour of her knickers (while she voluntarily announces all her sex secrets to his saintly brother Chuff) before they are called in by their thundering father's voice. In the second the brothers and their sister learn lessons in the repetitiveness of world history and, via geometry, some of the biological facts of life. In the third chapter the stories of the Norwegian Captain's marital entrapment by Kersse the Irish tailor and the shooting of the Russian General by the Irish soldier Buckley are told on the public-house radio and/or television sets, during a brawl that leaves the long-suffering publican/host to clear up the empties. In the fourth the love-story of Tristan and Isolde is told by four garrulous and voyeuristic old men.

The four chapters of the third book (III.i–iv) echo or contrast with many of the incidents in the first two. Shaun, beginning his backwards journey through the night, explains his role as postman, jibes at his brother and reveals at least the messages on the envelope of the letter he carries. In the next chapter, as Jaunty Jaun, he preaches erotically and ambiguously to the (at this point) twenty-nine girls, including his sister Izzy, who flock to him just as they have fled from his brother in II.i. As Pure Yawn he is more vigorously interrogated by the four old men. Others speak through him until the ghostly figure of his father makes his long-awaited speech of self-defence. In the fourth chapter the Porter family sleeps but the parents are awoken by the cries of Jerry (Shem) and, after a casuistical debate on the pros and cons, engage in a vigorous bout of middle-aged marital copulation (in their dream *alter egos* they are insects so the act is described in an extended pun as a game of crickets' cricket).

The fourth book celebrates the arrival of the dawn of a new day, a new modern age and a new political situation. New roles for the waking sons are glimpsed in brief pictures of the bath-tub isolation of St Kevin and of the Druid who debated with St Patrick for the soul of Ireland (according to Joyce the scene describes 'the conversion *of* St Patrick *by* Ireland' (to H.S.W. 3 August 1923, my italics)). The letter of vindication is finally revealed and the book closes with an invitation to the 'sonhusband' from his 'daughterwife' (*FW*, 627.1–2) to wake, only to rebegin again at the beginning.

THE COMPOSITION OF EVERYBODY

To make a narrative gloss of the book is not just to gloss over its Shandyan/Rushdiean digressiveness but to imply a whole series of readerly assumptions about 'wideawake language, cutandry grammar and goahead plot' that many would say it was the main purpose of Joyce's narrative to disrupt. There are implications about structure to be drawn from Joyce's letters, which describe his compositional progress in a series of often bizarre metaphors. One of the first and most important of these refers to his sketches as 'boring parties' tunnelling from two and then from several sides (*SL*, 304), 'hammering' at the elements in order to make them 'fuse themselves' together. This clearly non-sequential conception requires that even a plot summary of the book must in a quite literal way be understood as an interpretation or translation, and each reading may turn up different strategies of selection – even different senses of what might be said to be the plot.

The process of fusion can be seen in the way Joyce began by making notes on the historical/mythical figures of St Kevin, St Patrick and Tristan in his notebooks, figures that eventually merged into his warring brothers: the saintly ladies' man Shaun and the exiled lover

Shem (mixing Cain and Noah's Shem amd Ham). The Bloomian cuckold, King Mark, awkwardly present though usually somehow obscured in the traditional Romantic myth of Tristan and Isolde, fascinated Joyce and provided him with a base that developed into the 'four dear old heladies' (*FW*, 386.14–5) Matthew, Mark, Luke, John or Mamalujo, with or without their ass, that are the voyeur-narrators of II.iv, the interrogators of III.iii, the bedroom snoopers of III.iv, possibly multiply into the twelve bar customers and or jurors of II.i and II.iii, and the four-stage Viconian oral/Irish historians throughout.

Joyce's first sketch in March 1923 was a theatricalised parody on Rory O'Conor, the last king of Ireland before the Anglo-Norman invasion in the twelfth century, whose followers desert him like pub drinkers at closing time. Theatricalised parody or pastiche has been said by Stephen Heath (1984) to be the genre of these sketches and a dominant genre of the *Wake* itself. Many passages in the book bear this out, such as the parody of Juno's toilet from *Iliad* XIV in I.viii (*FW*, 206.29–207.20), that of Rowntree's survey of urban poverty in HCE's speech in III.iii (*FW*, 540–5) and of the florid Edgar Quinet passage about the survival of the flora despite historical change which is given in a form near its French original in II.ii (*FW*, 281.4–13) and translated into 'turfish' (*FW*, 281–2) in II.i (*FW*, 236.19–32) and elsewhere. 'Rory O'Conor' might be said to recall the parodic portraits of Irish heroes in the 'Cyclops' episode of *Ulysses*, but the sketch also seems to develop and extend the widely diverging stylistic trajectories of several if not all of the later episodes of the book at one and the same time. It is closest, perhaps, to the colloquial future-babble at the end of 'Oxen'. But then it is also more drunkenly surreal than 'Circe'; more digressive than 'Eumaeus'; more packed with information than 'Ithaca'; more associatively flowing than 'Penelope' and so on.

The sketch was composed out of left-over notes from *Ulysses*, like Rory's own activity of 'heeltapping' the empty glasses (*FW*, 381.09), elsewhere called 'executing . . . empties' (*FW*, 52.01–3). In it we can already see some of the traits and themes that were to be developed into the Earwicker figure whose odd name (suggesting awakener, earwig, Viking Eric and so on) Joyce picked up from a gravestone in Sidlesham Churchyard near Bognor where he stayed that summer. Rory is already a publican and something of an *Amalgamemnon* (to borrow the title of a recent Brooke-Rose novel): a composite of everyman and myth. Such an early effort fitted, with surprisingly little adaptation (beyond the addition of a couple of hce phrases and some further digressive expansion), into that last-composed chapter, prefiguring the process by which isolated incidents in the book can be read as versions of the one archetypal plot.

Undoubtedly the Brunonian law by which each thing may meet and merge into its opposite works to disrupt the 'neatness of identifications' that Beckett spotted as the biggest danger for both writer and reader engaged in this kind of method.

How, for instance do we align the Tailor and Captain story of II.iii to Earwicker? On the one hand the chains of polysemantic association lead us from Kersse (the tailor's name perhaps because he suffers the 'kersse' of the Captain 320.2, 12) to Persse (by remembering that the ancient Celtic languages divided into Brythonic and Goidelic branches according to their respective uses of P or K), thence to the Persse O'Reilly of the ballad in I.ii who, as the French for earwig is *perce oreille*, must be Earwicker. On the other hand we may link the errant Norwegian Captain to all things Scandinavian and, as future husband, to Viking invader and sex criminal paterfamilias Earwicker, who is undoubtedly himself the sartorial victim of some quite extraordinary costumes in I.ii (*FW*, 30.23–31.03 and 35.8–10), as Jarl van Hoother in I.i (*FW*, 22.34–23.03), as Rory (*FW*, 381.11–15) and so on.

Alternatively HCE may not be primarily related to either figure but only to the 'host' of the 'bottlefilled' (*FW*, 310.26), largely unnamed unless one accepts the name 'Burniface' (*FW* 315.09; Boniface was another of the odd names on graves in the Sidlesham churchyard). As publican he may count the money and therefore be the 'teller' at whom his wife 'winks' (*FW*, 310.29–30). The tailor may be the subject of a story broadcast on the pub radio or else he too may be the 'teller' of the tale. Joyce, signing himself 'Jeems Jokes' and '[(his mark)' seems to describe himself in a tailoring metaphor in his letters to Harriet Weaver about the commissioned sketch (*SL*, 316–18). Or else she may be winking at the tiller or rudder (as the 'teller' becomes, *FW*, 319.24) of the 'bugganeering' or roving 'nowedding captain' (*FW*, 325.27), which we presume to be hanging down beneath the bottom of his ship.

There is little or no agreement, however, about such identifications. According to McHugh (1976), the Captain and Tailor are to be identified rather as types of the warring brothers: erring Shem and stay-at-home Shaun. For Hart (1962) the Captain, as Norwegian speaker, is primarily connected to the barman-policeman figure Sistersen-Sigurdsen of I.vii and III.i. Any or all of these may have been the kinds of possibilities Joyce could keep simultaneously alive by the time his tunnelling process was complete.

Structurally the great cycle of the *Wake* is usually said to proceed in a four-stage progression based on the historical theory of Vico: a Viconian stage for the four books and for each group of four chapters within the books according to Tindall (1969), who himself admitted the loose working of such a scheme. For Hart its structure was first seen as a circular repetition of motifs, though this model proved too rigidly based on the high-Romantic Wagnerian example to cope with either the sequential or the more radically Brunonian elements that have subsequently been revealed. These, to borrow a phrase from particle physics, may more accurately be said to represent a Brownian motion of chaotically rebounding alternatives.

Since the *Wake* is a snake with its tail in its mouth, it might, in any case, make just as much sense to read it in a different kind of order, turning the epic author of *Ulysses* into the epic reader of the *Wake* by beginning, quite literally, *in medias res*. Why not begin with the 'Rory O'Conor' sketch that was the first passage composed? The reader would then be led gently into the world of the *Wake* through the chapter where the Four Old Men are telling the Tristan story (II.iv), preferably pausing to digest the ways in which it was composed by joining two of the others of Joyce's 1923 sketches together. The reader might note the origin of these sketches in a sort of theatricalised parody and the distance between that mode and the later version. And he or she might note from the outset the extent to which, in the foregrounding of its Mamalujo narrators (the four gospellers of the New Testament, authors of the *Four Annals* of Irish history, four waves, four provinces and so on), narration becomes as much the subject as the medium of the *Wake*. The idea that there may be separate identifiable narrative voices and that these voices may also be mixed would also be before the reader from the start. Next would come the relatively straightforward transformatory narrative of Shaun, Jaun, Yawn in book III. The new reader might pause to note, though probably not stay to work out in detail, the odd disintegrations of the hypnotised Shaun's voice before it bursts out clearly with HCE's speech. Then in the last chapter would come the Porters who provide the closest thing to a realistic narrative base. Most of book III was composed before 1926 and serialised in *transition* in 1928–9. The morning of book IV (incorporating further early sketches of Kevin, St Patrick and the letter) would lead naturally on to the wake/waking of Finnegan and the story of HCE in book I (which was drafted after the early sketch phase of composition and serialised in the first numbers of *transition* from April to November 1927).

Not until then would the reader be confronted with the denseness and difficulty of book II, with its teasing nightgames, puzzlingly ambiguous lessons and finally its almost impenetrably carnivalised and interrupted drunken pub-narratives of II.iii, which were, after all, the last sections of the book to be composed. After the Tailor and Captain conundrum in II.iii, we have a narrative of the shooting of the Russian General whose oral source (it was one of Joyce's father's favourite stories) is layered over with narrative dialogisation at least as complex as that of Stephen's parable in 'Aeolus'. It is told by the double act of Butt and Taff, on television, in the pub and interrupted by a horserace commentary, a television pope and a report of the splitting of the atom or 'etym'. In its context the story may add to its immediate Crimean War context the anti-Oedipal father–son incest mentioned as unmentionable by Stephen in 'Scylla and Charybdis' (Rabaté, 1991), an O'Casey-like play about the violent insurrection against the British in Ireland, the Russian Revolution, or the impending conflagration of the Second World War. Hardly any of book II was serialised until the middle and later part of the 1930s (1933, 35, 37 and 38). It gave Joyce the most trouble in composition and shows the *Wake*'s language at its most complex point of punning development.

By this means, in broad outline, the reader's experience of reading the book would follow Joyce's experience of writing it, with attention drawn to the early sketches that, with good Brunonian sense, Joyce incorporated at terminal points in the book. The search for meaning might be more closely tied to the genetic study that, with the *Wake*, so often accompanies it, giving the modern intentionalist critic a good grounding for his or her reading and allowing the narrative of the book to be realigned with the contexts in which it was produced.

THE YEARS OF THE UNDERGROUND

However complex its relation to them, and however decontextualising might be the effect of its universalising correspondences, the book's immediate contexts can and must be taken into account. In Joyce's life and political surroundings, the euphoria of the 1920s was succeeded by the tensions and anxieties of the 1930s and the *Wake*'s composition and its deeply doubled text represent the former crossed through and mixed with the latter. In 1923 Joyce was forty-one, with a seventeen-year-old son and a fifteen-year-old daughter. His artistic reputation was explosive but his health, and especially his eyesight, was in decline. An almost nomadic life – based in Paris but taking frequent recuperative trips elsewhere – had become the norm.

In Irish politics partition and the Irish Free State had been established in the year that *Ulysses* was first published. During the years of the *Wake*'s progress violent conflict in the south was gradually replaced by political conflict between the more moderate and more extreme independence parties, with de Valera's Fianna Fail gradually taking the ascendancy and leading the country to its new constitution in 1939 and to its neutrality in the Second World War: the 'devil era' referred to at the end of III.ii. The telegram reputedly sent by de Valera to the German people expressing sympathy for the death of their Chancellor in 1945 surely took that neutrality too far. Political power meant compromising extreme Republican ambitions and the underground, potentially violent, political activism of the IRA was born.

On the European and world stage, the Wall Street Crash of 1926 set a pattern of recurring economic crises that brought stark ideological divisions between left and right. In Russia in 1922 Stalin became General Secretary of the Communist Party, consolidating his position against all opposition, and eventually suspending collective government in 1934. In Britain, to the liberalisation implied by Irish independence, was added political ensuffragement for women (1918 and 1928) and greater social, educational and sexual freedom for all, which even allowed for the legal publication of *Ulysses* (United States, 1933; United Kingdom, 1936). But such progress had to be vigorously defended. In Germany democracy collapsed into Fascist militarism, plunging the developed world into war.

In the literary world, the energy of the avant-garde movement – centred in Paris – was strong and held sway in all the arts. Early modernist iconoclasm was being replaced by a maturer, even established, literary mode. Eliot moved to Anglicanism and *Four Quartets*; Woolf was writing *The Waves* (1931); and Lawrence's *Lady Chatterley's Lover* was completed only two years before his death (1930). One result of the triumph of these writers was, however, a fear that art was pursuing an increasing gnomic complexity for its own sake. There was felt to be a growing split between the artist and the social world. The institution of academic criticism might be said to have expanded to fill this gap. Leavis began *Scrutiny* in 1932. Paradoxically, literary avant-gardism may have invited both positively and by reaction more politically charged literary voices and more cultural populism to emerge.

In 1926 Baird demonstrated television, the first transmissions of which started before the Second World War. Telephone and radio were becoming familiar as means of communication and Joyce's text is quick to exploit their potential. Shaun's voice is like broadcasts from the 'marconimasts of Clifden' in III.i (*FW*, 407.20); the Norwegian Captain narrative of III.iii is broadcast on the publican's fully described 'tolvtubular high fidelity daildialler' (*FW*, 309.14) and the Butt and Taff dialogue which follows on his '*bairdboard bombardment screen*' (*FW*, 349.08); the letter is described as a 'radiooscillating epiepistle' (*FW*, 108.24). Patrick and the Druid may appear as details of a 'Velivision victor' (*FW*, 610.35); and Festy King and his accomplices are accused of taking assumed names from the 'tellafun book' (*FW*, 86.14).

The *Wake* continues and extends the sense established in *Ulysses* that the existence of these new media was being recognised and reflected at a deep level. The distorted, disembodied voices of the text and its eclectic 'magazine' mixtures of material both seem suggestive in this respect. As with *Ulysses*, we sense that the task of prose fiction is now more than ever to immerse itself so deeply in its medium that no translation into any other medium could ever reproduce more than a part of its richness or ever challenge the authentic character of its mediation.

The 1930s were a time of political authoritarianism and of secret oppositional confederacies in which underground movements flourished. In 1933 the London Underground railway was amalgamated into a single network, through whose simplified structure the anatomy of the city increasingly came to be understood. As Terence Brown has said, literary undergrounds were important too. While obscenity laws may have relaxed their strictures on his work, Joyce was taking no chances. His new semantics was another form of underground which provided that any amount of sexual indecency, of dangerous or subversive political reference, could be built into a structure the logic of whose ambiguity demanded that any perception of 'obscenity' be attributable to the depravity or corruption of the reader, rather than that of the author himself.

The loss of innocence implied by the appearance of such novels as Bowen's *The Death of the Heart* (1938) or Greene's *The Power and The Glory* (1940); the publication of such alternative classics as Flann O'Brien's *At Swim-Two-Birds* (1939) and Samuel Beckett's *Murphy* (1938) and the latter's decision to join the wartime French underground; the arrest, in 1939, of the young Brendan Behan in Liverpool; the death and Auden-elegised winter burial of Yeats in 1939; Auden's own flight to America and that of Brecht and the suicide of Walter Benjamin in 1940 all contribute to our sense that the *Wake* was published in 1939 on a cold dark day.

POST-DIFFERENTIAL EPISTEMOLOGY

The medium of the *Wake* is language, whose history, structures and communicative limits it both explores and extends in several directions at once. Basically in English (though a long way from the 'Basic English' into which part of the Anna Livia chapter was translated by C. K. Ogden in 1926) the *Wake* draws on more than sixty other languages and dialects. These include the obvious languages that Joyce used in his places of residence such as French, German and Italian as well as Irish Gaelic and a series of English, Anglo-Irish and other slangs, cants and pidgins, the Latin of his education, and the Norwegian-Danish language that he first taught himself in order to read Ibsen. To these are added such exotic species as Telugu and the Rhaeto-Romanic dialect, as well as other European and non-European languages such as Kiswahili, Albanian, Hindustani, Ainu and Sanskrit and such artificial mixtures as Esperanto and Volapuk mixed into the unique 'S.P.Q.R.ish' (*FW*, 229.07) that some call 'Wakese'.

The language of the *Wake*, from its de-apostrophised title onward, is most often said to be composed of puns, though it might more accurately be said to be a kind of composite or aggregate of neologisms and what Carroll's Humpty Dumpty calls 'portmanteau words', which encourage and facilitate an extraordinary 'three score and ten toptypsical readings' (*FW*, 20.15) of each linguistic unit. Many of its terms seem deliberately to mix apparently irreconcilable opposites (Heath, 1984). Its language has been seen as a modern system for containing as much information in as small a space as possible (Hart, 1962), but also as an edenic medium related to the 'root' or original languages discovered by philological and etymological researches in the interconnectedness of words (Bishop, 1986). For some modern feminists its 'gramma's grammer' (*FW*, 268.17) celebrates the bodily, the maternal, the pre-linguistic rhythms of echolalia and glossolalia; for others it offers a more worrying paradigm (Henke, 1990).

The reader's most secure prop against the collapse of meaning into irresolvably contrary alternatives at every stage is the reasonably conventional character of the *Wake*'s syntax. One sensible exercise when confronting a section of the text is to decide, as far as possible, on the subject and predicate of its grammatical sentence. This, as often as not, turns out to be a relatively simple (or at least a possible) exercise – akin to the experience of translating from a half-familiar foreign language. It is also reassuring to discover that this syntactic skeleton often closely conforms to Joyce's first drafts of his texts, now available in Garland facsimile and, since 1963, in David Hayman's transcribed form.

It would of course be wrong to say that the *Wake*'s syntax was entirely conventional. A glance at the single sentence, three pages in length, that would first greet our 'epic reader' in the thumbnail portrait of Rory O'Conor with which he or she might begin the book (*FW*, 380–2) is enough to demonstrate that on the syntactic base is built, by a series of parentheses, additions and digressions, a highly complex logical structure of deferral.

The main subject, named as 'King Roderick O'Conor' (*FW*, 380.12) is qualified by a long string of relative or other appositional clauses explaining who he was, then renamed (*FW*, 380.33) and requalified, in clauses defining the relevant occasion, before we arrive at the first main predicate ('he just went heeltapping through the winespilth', *FW*, 381.09). This is itself qualified until the subject is named for the third time (*FW*, 381.25) as he went to 'suck up . . . whatever surplus rotgut . . . was left' (*FW*, 381.30–2) and still the sentence continues till dawn breaks (*FW*, 382.10–11) and in a final restatement of the subject with a final predicate 'our wineman from Barleyhome he just slumped to throne' (*FW*, 382.26–7). Apposition is piled on apposition and parenthetical suspension of sense (parentheses elsewhere in the text are frequently interruptive as well as elaborative) is the norm. The three-page sentence (as the long sentence listing all the presents Anna Livia brings from her borrowed mailbag in I.viii, *FW*, 209–12, may hint) defines Joyce as a veritable Santa of the clause.

Nor is deferral always as easily closed off as it is at the end of this passage. Joyce frequently built a certain amount of ambiguity into his syntax in the course of his composition (or decomposition) of the book, such as the suggestion of the noun 'passenger' alongside the French '*pas encore*' in 'passencore', or the 'Rot a peck of pa's malt' that partially disrupts the flow of 'not yet' phrases in the first full paragraph of the book. Is 'bitts' a noun or a conjunction in 'Your rear gait's creakor human bitts your butts disagrees' (*FW*, 214.21–2)? Aside from the ubiquitous mutation of the proper and attributive names, titles and epithets that function as syntactic subjects, the subject too may disappear, like the arithmetically minded Franky (Kev–Shaun) who is disguised in the apparently adverbial 'frankily' (*FW*, 282.08) at the start of the geometry lesson in II.ii.

Reading different syntactic possibilities in the language requires us to keep in mind different levels of narrative meaning of the text. Direct speech, famously signalled by dashes throughout Joyce's writings may, in the *Wake*, be introduced by a colon and without indentation. Even where dashes are used, as in III.iii, it can be difficult or impossible to establish who it is who speaks.

Who is the 'he' who 'rises' in II.ii (*FW*, 240.05)? Is it the angelic Chuff whose rise has just been celebrated by the female choir? Or could it be his defeated brother Glugg who, we have just been told, is 'in his grave' (*FW*, 240.04) and ripe for resurrection and for his third attempt on the secret colour riddle? Or else, as we begin to realise, it may be their father, still apparently within the house, but setting about his evening chores and about to summon in the children from play.

The possibilities presented by pronouns for the suspension of meaning are, as in 'Penelope', exploited to the full.

Clustering of terms is another well-known feature of the language. In addition to the thousands of river names in I.vi, the *Wake* is consistently decorated with clusters of terms from some special area of interest or knowledge that the reader will typically note. Thousands of song and book titles and references to everything from cricket (*FW*, 583–4) to the types or 'orders' of angels (*FW*, 605–6) jostle in such clusters on the pages. For Tindall the activity of noting them is contemptuously known as 'birdwatching' but it is an essential part of reading the book. Bird names themselves (such as those that cluster in the passsage from Jaun's Lent sermon in III.ii, *FW* 449, that was glossed by Stuart Gilbert in *Our Exagmination*, or those that swarm around Yawn's mound in III.iii, *FW*, 478–9) are far from negligible or merely decorative in the *Wake*. They link up in the associative chains of meaning to the hen of I.v. According to Viconian theory, the Roman practice of 'auspices' or the reading of patterns of bird flight is merely the 'Divine Age' original of later written forms of Roman law.

Such clusterings help develop the role of the book as a post-modern encyclopaedia: that is an encyclopaedia which, unlike the classic Enlightenment project of encyclopaedism, defines and collates things not according to their differences but according to multiple and shifting correspondences, cross-correspondences and networkings of a kind that is only, perhaps, imaginable in the computer age. In this sense Joyce's act of theatricalised parody can be usefully understood as a theatricalised parody of the eleventh *Britannica*, which was often his first point of reference in composing the *Wake*.

Some readings of the *Wake* imply that the complexities created by its language are merely accidential: incoveniences beyond which the reader must pass as speedily as possible to find the true sense. For others they are structural and open up new possibilities for multiple reference or for the achievement of 'things unattempted yet in prose or rhyme'. Still others (including Beckett and post-structuralists like Attridge and Rabaté) suggest that the *Wake* language and its ambiguities deliberately prevent any realisation of a represented fictional world. Even an interpretationist like Tindall (1959) wrote that the *Wake* is 'about itself'. Beckett (1929) had written more subtly that 'it is not about something it is that something itself'.

One gloss on this important post-modern idea is that the book itself
is implicitly or explicitly discussed in the frequent discussions of
language, texts (the letter), authorship (Shem) and mediation (Shaun)
that occur throughout the text (Benstock, 1965). Furthermore the
experience of the reader and the act of reading are repeatedly evoked
in the *Wake* whose very opacity, as so frequently with post-modern
texts, lends further weight to its being read as self-referential both to
itself and to types of reader response.

> (Stoop) if you are abcedminded, to this claybook, what curios of
> signs (please stoop), in this allaphbed!   (*FW*, 18.17–18)

In I.v, in examining the letter, this passage from I.i is developed and
four distinguishable types of reader and of reading are imagined, from
the 'naif alphabetters' who find it the work of a 'recidivist' to the
'hardily curiosing entomophilust' to whom it is 'a very sexmosaic of
nymphosis'. 'Closer inspection . . . would reveal a multiplicity of
personalities' which may 'coalesce' 'under the closed eyes of the
inspectors' into 'one stable somebody'. I.v is a chapter about the
interpretation of texts, like the *Book of Kells*, the description of whose
'Tunc' page by Sir Edward Sullivan provides the base for Joyce's
parody on pages 119–23. The complex textual history of sacred texts
like the Bible and the Koran is at once parodied in and claimed for the
Wake itself. The four old men narrators of II.iv themselves become
interrogators and interpreters in III.iii and ones whose voiced
puzzlement about the voices emanating from the hypnotised Yawn
stimulates or echoes that of the destabilised reader who may agree
with the bog Latin accusation: '*Magis megis enerretur mynus hoc
intelligow*', the more it is interpreted, the less it is understood (*FW*,
478.17–18). The twelve pub customers of II.iii and witnesses and
jurors of I.iv and III.iii are also interpreters, both anticipating and
incorporating the first critics of the *Our Exagmination* volume that
was published in 1929 when the completion of the book was still ten
years away. Both Shem (*FW*, 179.24–180.30) and HCE/Porter (*FW*,
356.19–358.16) are shown as readers possibly of the same
'(suppressed) book'. Finnegan's resurrection is, among other things,
an image of what one critic of *Ulysses* called the reader's 'many happy
returns' to the book (Thomas, 1982). The meta-dialogical levels
glimpsed in the 'Aeolus' episode of *Ulysses* become, as in a post-

modern meta-fiction like Italo Calvino's *If On a Winter's Night a Traveller* (1979), the substance of much of the text.

Nothing less than the history of writing is glimpsed in references to such kinds of writing as the runic 'Futhorc' (*FW*, 018.34), monumental 'ogham' (*FW*, 123.08), ideogrammatic 'letterwords' (*L*, I 250), 'hieroglyph' (*FW*, 122.07), and scripts that run 'furrowards, bagawards, like yoxen at the turnpaht' (*FW*, 18.32). They are both mentioned and aped in the *Wake*, which includes its 'sigla' (*FW*, 299 n 4), as well as the rotating 'E' (*FW*, 006.32, 036.17 and 119.17) and 'fretful fidget F' (*FW*, 120.33, 121.03,07 and 266.22) among the elements in its typographical repertoire. Messages, their secretive authors, their often unwitting messengers and their constant interrogation and examination make up much of the book's commentary on the possibilities of its own meaning and on the history of its own composition.

Yet the horizons of possible communication seem to be always within view. The *Wake*'s post-modernity, in Lyotard's much-used formula, 'puts forward the unpresentable in presentation itself.' Its language of punning, more than just a 'joke' or 'experiment', may imply a whole new epistemology, a new way of understanding a world of unexpected analogies and far-reaching syntheses, beyond the national, linguistic and conceptual boundaries that establish traditional forms of difference (Norris, 1974). If language, as Saussurians argue, is difference, then the *Wake* must be 'nat language at any sinse of the world' (*FW*, 83.12).

This epistemology is one that anticipates and enacts the defeat of tyrannical Fascism in the Second World War. With its post-colonial development of Asian, Australasian, African and American subtexts, it looks forward, beyond Europe, to whole-world understandings in a global future. If *Ulysses* is a mocking epic of Christo-Judaic secularism, then the *Wake* envisions a secular Joydaehindchrislam-buddhist universalism and beyond. Language and writing become both the subject and the tool of this new epistemology: a new, pan-synoptical, language-based world view for the contemporary urban secular mentality, which is announced as an 'epistlemadethemology for deep dorfy doubtlings' (*FW*, 374.17–18).

The prospect of a language as mixed and fluid as that of the *Wake* induces sharp panic in traditionalists who wonder what effect it might have if it ever leaked into more general use. We may find, in a passage of I.v, such issues pre-emptively discussed. An interrogator of the 'mamafesta' asks what would happen if 'the lingo gasped between kicksheets, however basically English, were to be preached from the mouths of wickerchurchwardens and metaphysicians' (*FW*, 116.25–7)? He continues to ask 'where would their practice be or where the human race itself were the Pythagorean sesquipedalia of the panepistemion, however apically Volapucky, grunted and grom-welled . . . over country stiles?' (*FW*, 116.25–33). One level of the answer that is apparently given is that language has always been so mixed and adulterated: 'So hath been, love: tis tis: and will be' (*FW*, 116.36).

All language and culture and their deep structures, not just the obvious legally, politically and morally established formulae, might be thought of as controlling or determining men and women as social subjects. Such seems to be the implication of Stephen's speculations on names and fates in *A Portrait* and *Ulysses*, and the view has gained much ground in the social and linguistic theories of Foucault, Lacan, modern feminism, Said and Bhabha's post-colonialism and so on. Joycean polysemy might be seen as a deliberate resistance to this phenomenon. In sexual terms, for instance, Krafft-Ebing's nineteenth-century taxonomy of differing sexual orientations was designed to assist the criminalisation of the abnormal or deviant practice: an assumption not entirely absent from Freudian psychoanalytic practices of treatment and cure. But the *Wake*'s pan-Oedipalisation of language (its mixture of normal and perverse modes of sexuality and its insistence on the multiplicity of incestuous desires within its family) makes criminalisation and control seem out of place.

What boundaries or inhibitions the book's epistemology proposes to these or other kinds of knowledge and freedom – beyond the ever-expanding limits of human potential – is still, as yet, unclear. In part this may be one of the paradoxical results of the manner in which we have come to understand it. Inevitably, much of that understanding has been to define the book's world in terms of that which preceded it, in terms of those things out of which it was built. In the case of Joyce this activity alone requires that we compile a new kind of encyclo-paedia. But a further kind of reading might pay attention to the novelty that may be created from these materials but not contained by them, to those new things that the language of the *Wake* describes that have not yet come into the world. The well-known use of the *Wake*'s 'quark' (previously a German word for soft cheese and used in II.iv as an onomatopoeic representation of a seagull's call) as the term for the newly discovered subatomic particle, provides one such example. How many more Wakean neologisms might we find meaningful not only as combinations of already existing things from the past but as terms for things that we do not yet know to exist?

ANAMORPHIC HYPOTHESES

A bucket of cold water was thrown on all this by F. R. Leavis, in his 1933 review of the early instalments of the *Wake* and its *Exagmination* supporters, declaring *Finnegans Wake* to be 'not worth the labour of reading'. It would be folly to underestimate that labour but, for a critic like Parrinder, writing some fifty years later, 'the rewards of reading the *Wake* are immense'. Leavis disapproved of the vaunted idea that in the *Work in Progress* 'the interest in words and their possibilities come first'. He found Joyce's orderings 'mechanical' and un-Shakespearean. But Joyce's linguistic self-consciousness has amply proved its importance, and to many readers *Finnegans Wake* is as much like theatre – especially Shakespearean theatre – as any prose narrative could be. The 'culture of leisure' that Leavis anticipated but distrusted has to some extent come about and made an enlarged space for Joyce. So too has the increasing phenomenon of work in the cultural sphere. Increasing cultural syntheses have also helped provide a more sympathetic environment for Joyce's experiment.

Despite Leavisite and other scowling voices, criticism of the *Wake* has proceeded vigorously on all fronts with glosses and indexes revealing more and more of the detail of the work's pun possibilities. With many glosses having been collected together in McHugh's *Annotations to Finnegans Wake* (1980), new horizons of Wakean readability have been reached and much is now possible for the keen private reader that would previously have been impossible outside a major university library. Research into textual genesis, culminating in the facsimile reproduction of Joyce's manuscripts, drafts and

notebooks in 1984, has continued to reveal more and more of the logic
and machinery of the book's composition (Hayman, 1991).

Critical theory and method and our understandings of language and
cultural context have continued to be tested out on and to try to keep
pace with the *Wake*. On the other hand, many of the everyday ideas
and asociations that would have been obvious to Joyce and his
immediate associates may now have been lost forever.

Joyce's notebooks remain, as yet, largely untranscribed and
unannotated in full, though their complete assimilation seems now
within view. A completely re-edited text of the book, with all the
difficulties that implies, may also soon become available.

The legacy of Leavisism may not be the only reason why many
readers still come to the *Wake* and suffer disappointments. No doubt
the expectations that certain readers bring to the text have something
to do with it too. Many seem to base their reading on implied
anamorphic hypotheses about the text. According to such hypotheses,
Wakean complexity is only a superficial kind of distortion, like that of
anamorphic pictures or writing whose distortion disappears when they
are viewed from a certain perspective or reflected in a correctively
distorting mirror.

But Wakean distortion or decomposition is not quite of this
superficial kind and any such approach to it is only likely to
demonstrate the circularity of its own hermeneutics. The language of
the *Wake* operates according to its own laws, which are, as yet, only
partly understood and which may require, at the very least, multiple or
synthetic perspectives to be simultaneously applied to them.

It is, furthermore, a system that declares itself to include what are
normally thought of as forms of chaos or of error. It includes Joyce's
famous answer to the knock on the door of his Paris flat that was taken
down in dictation and included into the text (Ellmann, 1982, p. 649)
(though no one has yet traced it among the versions of 'come in' and
'*entrez*' that abound). That there are 'miscegenations on miscegenations' (*FW*, 18.20); that 'papyr is meed of, made of, hides and
hints and misses in prints' (*FW*, 20.10–11); that the letter was 'Opened
by Miss Take' (*FW*, 420.26); that Shaun 'misunderstruck an aim for an
ollo' in three of the questions of I.vi (*FW*, 126.7–8); and that HCE has
been massively 'Missaunderstaid' (*FW*, 363.36) is not always
sufficiently understood.

According to Joyce's psychopathology of everyday life, and built into the first page of his book, the Christian Church was founded on the Greek pun on Peter's name in Matthew 16.18. In Joyce's version, the Eden story shows the whole world to have been built out of the 'happy fault' of human sexual sin. Error is built into and not excluded from the 'chaosmos' of Joyce's work, and it is to be hoped that the new interest in the theory and causality of chaos among modern mathematicians and physicists will help us to sketch more accurately the trails of Wakean chaos emanating from simple signs, like the expanded peacock tail of mathematical calculations noticed by Stephen in *A Portrait* (*P*, 106).

If the *Wake* is to be seen as the '1000th generation computer' suggested by Jacques Derrida (1984), then it is one that needs to be understood, not according to our anamorphic hypotheses, but as what has been called by progammers a 'counter-intuitive' system that forces us to reconsider the assumptions we bring to it, however common-sensical, however ideologically correct, however 'sesquipedalian' they might have seemed to be.

In this way the *Wake* brings to its culmination a tendency implicit in all Joyce's works. It is a profoundly anti-ideological book and one that makes the hermeneutic circularity implicit in our attempts to understand it more fully explicit than they seem to be elsewhere. How valuable it might be to evolve a critical language as knowledgeable, as inclusive and yet as fundamentally sceptical about its own achievements as the semi-parodic academic languages in which this text explains itself. Such a language would avoid the inevitable reductions of critical metalanguage and inapplicability of all labels, even deconstructive labels, to its working. Until then the least constrictive assessments such as that by Margot Norris that the *Wake* 'measures our capacity for intellectual adventure' or by Jacques Derrida that it 'mobilizes the totality of the equivocal' are among the most resonant formulations of its achievement.

Advances in computer technology and their harnessing may hold out more hope than any single critical formulation for the advancement of our learning about *Finnegans Wake*. It is now possible to imagine, if not yet to produce, a machine-readable text that might offer on-screen information, by means of colour highlighting and windowing facilities (keyed to units of sub-morpheme, morpheme, phrase, cluster, sentence, paragraph, sub-narrative and chapter length) of a variety of different kinds of information.

These should include: (1) access to the various genetic levels of the text including early published versions and drafts; (2) some kind of continuous early version akin to David Hayman's; (3) references where possible back to notebook entries and even source texts from which the entries were derived; (4) the polyglossary to all languages known to have been used by Joyce, which was first envisioned by Brendan O'Hehir, including a full cross-referencing with the *OED*; (4) an accumulating list of glosses of the kind collected by Roland McHugh, but systematically backed up with full information of an encyclopaedia-entry type and thoroughly credited to the first discoverer where possible; (5) special references to those passages whose glosses were given by Joyce or under his supervision; (6) an index of the *Wake*'s self-cannibalisations, perhaps based on Hart's index of recurrent motifs; (7) an index of Joyce's cannibalisations of and references to his own earlier works; (8) the cross-referencing from the text to available critical arguments based on sections of it that has been suggested by Fritz Senn (1982); (9) a form of syntactic simplification, of the kind outlined above in relation to the Rory O'Conor sketch, to assist the reader's construction of narrative continuum and context.

This 'rainbow' or 'chameleon' computer text might begin to bring the totality of the book into view and capture something like the full potential of its 'millwheeling vicociclometer' which:

> receives through a portal vein the dialytically separated elements of precedent decomposition for the verypetpurpose of subsequent recombination so that the heroticisms, catastrophes and eccentricities transmitted by the ancient legacy of the past . . . [can be] . . . anastomisically assimilated and preteridentified paraidiotically . . . (*FW*, 614.27–615.06)

Post-modern fictions, from Julian Barnes's *A History of the World in 10 1/2 Chapters* to Julian Rios's *Larva*, imply that each book now must be a kind of Noah's Ark from whose carefully selected elements past cultures could be reconstituted in some distant dreaded future in which cultural survival is by no means guaranteed. This computer *Wake*, as the Wake's own metaphorical computer, may guarantee that:

the samebold, gamebold adomic structure of our Finnius the old One, as highly charged with electrons as hophazards can effective it, may be there for you, Cockalooralooraloomenos, when cup, platter and pot come piping hot, as sure as herself pits hen to paper and there's scribblings scrawled on eggs. (*FW*, 615.6–10).

READING LIST

James A. Atherton, *The Books at the Wake* (New York: Viking, 1960).

Samuel Beckett *et al.*, *Our Exagmination Round his Factification for Incamination of Work in Progress* (1929) (London: Faber, 1961).

Michael Begnal, *Dreamscheme* (Syracuse: Syracuse University Press, 1988).

Michael Begnal and Grace Eckley, *Narrator and Character in Finnegans Wake* (Lewisburg: Bucknell University Press, 1975).

Pieter Bekker, 'Reading *Finnegans Wake*', in *James Joyce and Modern Literature*, ed. W. J. McCormack and A. Stead (London: Routledge, 1982) pp. 185–201.

Bernard Benstock, *Joyce-Again's Wake* (Seattle: University of Washington Press, 1965).

John Bishop, *Joyce's Book of the Dark* (Madison: University of Wisconsin Press, 1986).

Joseph Campbell and Henry Morton Robinson, *A Skeleton Key to Finnegans Wake* (London: Faber, 1947).

Vincent Cheng, *Shakespeare and Joyce: A Study of Finnegans Wake* (Dublin: Colin Smythe, 1984).

Jack P. Dalton and Clive Hart (eds), *Twelve and a Tilly* (London: Faber, 1966).

Jacques Derrida, 'Two Words for Joyce', in Attridge and Ferrer (1984) pp. 145–159.

Adaline Glasheen, *Third Census of Finnegans Wake* (California: University of California Press, 1977).

John Gordon, *Finnegans Wake: A Plot Summary* (Dublin: Gill and Macmillan, 1986).

Clive Hart, *Structure and Motif in Finnegans Wake* (London: Faber, 1962).

David Hayman, *A First-Draft Version of Finnegans Wake* (London: Faber, 1963).

David Hayman, *The 'Wake' in Transit* (Ithaca: Cornell University Press, 1991).

Stephen Heath, 'Ambiviolences', in Attridge and Ferrer (1984) pp. 31–68.

F. R. Leavis, 'James Joyce and "The Revolution of the Word"', *Scrutiny*, vol. 2 (1933) no.1, pp. 193–201.

Roland McHugh, *The Sigla of Finnegans Wake* (London: Edward Arnold, 1976).

Roland McHugh, *Annotations to Finnegans Wake* (London: Routledge, 1980).

Louis Mink, *A Finnegans Wake Gazetteer* (Bloomington: Indiana University Press, 1978).

Margot Norris, *The Decentered Universe of Finnegans Wake* (Baltimore: Johns Hopkins University Press, 1974).

Margot Norris, 'Finnegans Wake', in Attridge (1990).

Denis Rose and John O'Hanlon, *Understanding Finnegans Wake* (New York: Garland, 1982).

Fritz Senn, 'A Modest Proposal', *James Joyce Broadsheet*, no. 7 (1982) p. 3.

James Snead, 'Some Prefatory Remarks on Character in Joyce', in Benstock (1988) pp. 139–147.

Brook Thomas, *James Joyce's "Ulysses": A Book of Many Happy Returns* (Baton Rouge: Louisiana State University Press, 1982).

William York Tindall, *A Reader's Guide to Finnegans Wake* (London: Thames and Hudson, 1969)

Edmund Wilson, 'The Dream of H. C. Earwicker' in *The Wound and the Bow* (London: Methuen, 1961) pp. 218–43.

Index of References and Themes

Index of Characters

This index is designed to provide easy access to parts of the text for readers familiar with traditional narrative but should not be allowed to obscure the complex critical issues involved in establishing what is or is not a 'character', especially in *Finnegans Wake*.